G. A. Lethbridge Banbury

Sierra Leone

The white man's Grave

G. A. Lethbridge Banbury

Sierra Leone
The white man's Grave

ISBN/EAN: 9783743317451

Manufactured in Europe, USA, Canada, Australia, Japa

Cover: Foto ©ninafisch / pixelio.de

Manufactured and distributed by brebook publishing software (www.brebook.com)

G. A. Lethbridge Banbury

Sierra Leone

SIERRA LEONE:

OR,

THE WHITE MAN'S GRAVE.

SIERRA LEONE;

OR,

THE WHITE MAN'S GRAVE.

BY

G. A. LETHBRIDGE BANBURY.

LONDON:
SWAN SONNENSCHEIN & Co.,
PATERNOSTER SQUARE.

1889.

PREFACE.

AT the present day, when the reading world has before it the exciting histories and adventures, both true and mythical, of men who have travelled far and wide in the vast depths of the "Dark Continent," it seems pretentious to hope that much attention will be given to the following pages. But the writer does not launch this book as one of travel over unknown ground, nor as one of dangerous adventures and hardships. He simply aims at bringing before his readers a description of an Englishman's life in the most interesting but deadly colony of Sierra Leone.

The following pages first appeared in a series of private letters, and, having through death again fallen into the writer's hands, he presents them with humble apologies to his readers.

For him, life on the West Coast possessed a peculiar attraction only eclipsed by an ardent longing to go further afield, and penetrate into the vast unknown regions of this still unexplored land. He therefore trusts that this description in narrative form of that life, with its sunshine and shadow, its semi-civilization and occasional adventures, may not only possess a certain amount of interest, but give his kind readers an insight into the condition of affairs in "THE WHITE MAN'S GRAVE" a century after it was first populated by a few Englishmen and a band of liberated slaves.

G. A. L. BANBURY.

SHANKLIN, I.W.

CONTENTS.

CHAPTER		PAGE
I.	THE VOYAGE	1
II.	MADEIRA AND THE CANARIES	7
III.	AN ADVENTURE AT SEA	18
IV.	GOREE AND THE GAMBIA	27
V.	NATIVE PECULIARITES, AND A TORNADO	44
VI.	EARLY HISTORY OF THE SETTLEMENT	56
VII.	SIERRA LEONE UNDER THE CROWN	67
VIII.	EARLY IMPRESSIONS	82
IX.	AN UNPLEASANT ENCOUNTER	98
X.	A FIGHT WITH AN ALLIGATOR	112
XI.	ALLIGATORS STILL	122
XII.	ALLIGATORS AND WATERLOO	134
XIII.	A GENERAL DESCRIPTION OF FREETOWN	145
XIV.	THE TRADE OF THE COLONY	164
XV.	ANNEXATIONS AND CUSTOMS	176
XVI.	A SAD CASE, AND NATIVE OATHS	191
XVII.	AN UNFORTUNATE HISTORY	202
XVIII.	A "LEOPARD" ADVENTURE	216
XIX.	A LOKKOH PALAVER AND DANCE	231
XX.	GENERAL EVENTS	242
XXI.	EXPEDITION IN SHERBRO AND BATTLE OF TALLIAH	256
XXII.	A GHOST—SNAKES—AND UNPLEASANT DUTIES	275
XXIII.	HOMEWARD BOUND	290

SIERRA LEONE.

CHAPTER I.

THE VOYAGE.

WHY I went to Sierra Leone is neither here nor there: perhaps I took that step from that insatiable wish "to see the world" which so ardently possesses many Englishmen; or perhaps I was actuated by an ambitious desire of obtaining promotion in a service in which success is popularly supposed to come specially to those who depart from the beaten track in search of it. However, I found myself one morning leaving the handsome building in Whitehall, devoted to Indian, Foreign and Colonial Affairs, engaged to go to Sierra Leone as a Government official, having entered its doors but a short while previously as one of those beings who are erroneously believed to play at Government work in dutiful unison with the fountains in Trafalgar Square.

The remaining days before departure passed only too rapidly in making purchases for my future home, and in receiving hospitable attentions which took the inevitable shape of farewell dinners kindly given by friends and brother officers, to speed the parting guest. By some of them I was looked upon as a lucky dog; by others—and I must admit a considerable majority—as taking a step not only hazardous but unnecessarily foolish. This opinion was expressed in many different ways. One kind friend, more facetious than the rest, observed that, inasmuch as I was bound for such a deadly place, it would only be judicious to include a coffin in my equipment, since it might come in handy at an early date; while, to add an uncomfortably realistic appearance to this considerately thoughtful forecast, innumerable mournful epitaphs, penned with the usual amount of lugubrious wit, were thrown in by way of cheerful accompaniment.

A friend who had travelled in Africa advised me in selecting my outfit. It seemed to give him special delight to inspect the numerous contrivances supposed by outfitters to be essential to those travellers who are bound for out-of-the-way places. My friend's inquisitiveness, when overhauling these ingenious inventions, generally ended in a satisfied smile when the obsequious attendant, who had pulled all manner of instruments out of a cunningly-arranged basket in the delusive hope of having found a purchaser, became visibly embarrassed in finding considerable difficulty in replacing them.

A varied collection of this kind of equipment may be seen at a well-known establishment in Cornhill. When we visited this store, my friend, in pursuit of his usual hobby, appeared to be particularly interested in a small hamper, ingeniously fitted so as to hold plates, tumblers, knives, forks, and spoons, a frying-pan, and camp-kettle, and many other things supposed to be invaluable to travellers.

"Capitally arranged," said my friend.

"Indeed it is, sir. And we have a great demand for them," replied the unsuspecting attendant, scenting a possible purchaser.

"Yes, I daresay you *do* sell a great number. This one appears to be very compact : but kindly allow me to see you replace all the articles; for I should like to see how they fit."

The attendant was fairly up to his work, and after one or two jambs, managed to complete the somewhat trying task.

"Very good—and lined with green baize, I observe. But is this basket waterproof?" was the next inquisitorial demand.

"Oh yes, sir, quite showerproof."

"Waterproof, I said," drily interposed my friend. "Because, if not, I am afraid it is of little use. Apart from that, I can assure you a real campaigner would find all these things unnecessary. For a picnic up the Thames, or for a volunteer encampment, they are doubtless excellent; but for actual work in the bush, or for the rough life of a sportsman, they are worse than useless."

However, we purchased other things, which compensated for our want of appreciation of these faddish but expensive articles.

The railway journey to Liverpool, where it was of couse raining, and the incidental confusion unavoidable upon such a busy landing wharf as Prince's Stage, where porters, emigrants, wealthier passengers, and agonised friends jostle one another amidst a confusion of bags and boxes, in their frenzied exertions of arrival and departure, needs only passing mention. At last, with other passengers, I am safely transferred to the British and African steamer "Senegal," already blowing off volumes of steam, as a fretful complaint at being still secured to her river moorings.

After taking possession of my cabin, and making friendly arrangements for our mutual comfort with the stranger who was to share it with me, I entered the saloon. Among my fellow passengers I observed a negro, dressed in the height of fashion, still adhering to the silk hat of civilization, and loth to remove the yellow kids covering his ebon hands. He was accompanied on board by three pretty English girls, determined to see the last of him, who vied with each other in showing themselves solicitous for his future welfare. As a parting souvenir, one produced an elaborately worked smoking cap, which this sable Adonis, nothing abashed, immediately donned: the others presented him with a pair of slippers and an embroidered scarf. These gifts of his fair friends, delayed to the last moment, created considerable interest among such of the other passengers as were not themselves engaged in the sad duty of bidding good-bye to friends and relatives.

But the luggage was now on board; the last warning bell clanged forth; a stentorian voice demanded if there were "Any more for the shore?" The final hand-clasps were exchanged, with their hearty meanings of love or friendship; and the tug steamed back to the landing-stage with handkerchiefs waving a sad farewell, while the "Senegal," in charge of the pilot, dropped slowly down the Mersey—outward bound for "The White Man's Grave."

CHAPTER II.

MADEIRA AND THE CANARIES.

THE first few days at sea, and the trying ordeal most landsmen undergo, are best passed over in silence. On the seventh morning, after an uneventful passage through the dreaded Bay of Biscay, Madeira was sighted; and the beauty of the island, as we rapidly approached it, created unspeakable delight, enhanced by the pleasurable anticipation of a run on shore.

The sun had not long risen; and as the morning clouds slowly ascended, ridge after ridge of picturesque country became exposed to our view. Dotted here and there on the hill-sides were numerous *cintras* (the name given to the houses on the hills), half hidden in dense foliage, now brightly shining in the morning sun, anon buried in a wafting cloud; while the courses of many small mountain-torrents could be plainly traced, wending their foaming, impetuous way to the ocean. The bold hills forming the background threw sombre shadows over the deep clefts separating the numerous lofty summits, and added to the grandeur of the charming tableau.

We were to stay here six hours: so parties were soon made to ride up the steep and slippery streets to the monastery on the hill. From this we descended in small hand sleighs, at a rapid rate, deftly steered by guides, who with one foot on the sleigh, and using the other to steer with, brought us back to the town. This novel method of travelling, which has a most exhilarating effect, has been adopted owing to the style of paving probably unknown elsewhere. The streets are made by driving sharp flints into the surface with the points uppermost, and carefully laid above the ground level. Traffic over these stones has produced a highly slippery surface, extremely dangerous to pedestrians; but they are laid sufficiently apart to enable horses to maintain a somewhat precarious foothold. Their broken hoofs, however, show the serious damage they sustain from this peculiar kind of roadmaking. No

THE "CAB" OF MADEIRA.

wheeled vehicles can be used in these slippery streets; and, in consequence, the traffic is carried on by means of sleighs with iron-bound runners.

A most primitive and inexpensive plan of carting merchandise is used. It consists of a thick plank, clamped with iron, with a slight bedding on its upper edges, so as to raise the goods still further from the ground. These planks are drawn up and down the slippery streets by teams of oxen, which appear to understand the different orders shouted by the "oxeteers" in no measured terms, and frequently emphasized by blows from their long sticks.

When it is necessary to stop these planks in their descent, they are pulled sideways, and the driver jumps on behind. To turn a sharp corner seems more difficult, since the plank slides a considerable distance in the wrong direction until the progress of the bullock takes it along the intended road. Oxen also do service in a much more elaborate sleigh, heavily canopied, to protect the occupants from the sun. These are the "cabs" of Madeira.

We visited the convent, where most beautifully constructed feather-flowers and Madeira lace, the work of the nuns, can be purchased. These were passed for our inspection through a double-barred grating, the money being pushed back in the same way to the ancient nun, who was thus carefully protected in her intercourse with the outer world.

In the streets we were followed by a pestering crowd of beggars, suffering from most unsightly maladies, which they persistently thrust before us with clamorous appeals for alms. But these wretches fade into insignificance in comparison with the diseases and deformities of others who haunt the doors of the numerous churches, and whose condition is so hopeless that they are unable to follow us in pursuit of their precarious calling. At the gaol windows, also, a mass of shock-headed human beings—to whom an outward application of water must have been unknown for many a day—fought for a front position, in the hope of obtaining a copper, for which they begged in no less piteous terms than the lame, the halt, and the blind. We were also harassed by a crowd of youths, imploring us, whenever we stopped for a single instant, to take the change in English silver, and give them gold in exchange, "to make earrings," they will say; but we soon learnt that they were employed by the numerous shopkeepers bent upon realising the heavy exchange the bank allows for gold coinage.

All the exhortations of our guide, whom we honoured by christening "Fergusson," were unavailing in keeping off this pestering horde; and we gladly sought refuge in one of the excellent hotels, to escape from their importunities. Here a capital luncheon was served, but its enjoyment was marred by the sickly appearance of most of the visitors, whose abnormally bright eyes and hectic complexions told the piteous tale of the fatal lingering disease with which they were vainly striving to contend. Though a warm summer's day, the windows and doors were closed, and side by side sat invalids suffering from consumption in all its sad stages—from the slight cough of those still buoyed with hope of cure—alas! never destined to be realised—to the dull, hollow, hacking sound emanating from others whose attenuated features and reduced figures showed but too surely that the sand-glass of their lives had nearly run.

After leaving Madeira, our course lay southward for two days, through calm seas and under azure skies, when we sighted Teneriffe, the most important of the Canary Islands. The Peak, clothed in perennial snow, loomed grandly in the distance, surrounded by other lofty hills, above which it majestically towers. We shortly anchored in the excellent harbour; and the town of Santa Cruz, with its shining white houses, lies smiling before us, while the cochineal plantations may be plainly traced, running in picturesque terraces up the gentle ascending slopes. The culture of the cochineal, however, threatens soon to be an industry of the past, as chemical research has led to the discovery of cheaper means of producing the dye hitherto made from these little insects.

It happened to be a fête day in the island; so we landed in force, and attended the gardens, where a Spanish military band was playing. The Spanish girls were in gala dress, but to our surprise they were mostly decked out in Parisian finery—the graceful mantilla, so becoming to them, being nowadays discarded for the modern hat, with its hybrid decorations of feathers and bows, and its fantastic vagaries in shape and substance.

Teneriffe is not inundated with the swarm of visitors that annually crowd to Madeira in the winter months. Any invalids who prefer keeping out of the beaten track, or wish to enjoy thorough rest, can find in Orotavo—a town situated on the opposite side of the Island to Santa Cruz—a charming place at which an enjoyable holiday can be spent at moderate cost. In Santa Cruz we visited the Cathedral, where the colours taken from Lord Nelson, when he made his gallant, but unsuccessful attempt to storm the island in 1797, are carefully preserved in a stout case. These flags were, until recently, suspended from one of the cathedral aisles, unguarded by lock and key, until an English middy, carried away by his loyal feelings, successfully accomplished the bold feat of recapturing them. This act created much excitement at the time, but after considerable diplomatic correspondence with the Spanish Government the flags were restored, and the young officer, for his plucky act, received a severe official reprimand.

There was a travelling company at the theatre, and as the "Senegal" could not leave before morning, we took a box. One of the pieces was the Spanish version of "Ici on parle Francais." This was followed by a ballet, introducing the graceful Fandango. As Englishmen, we loudly applauded this national dance, and demanded an encore, much to the gratification of the audience. As a mark of their appreciation at our expressed satisfaction, the band, among other *morceaux*, contributed "God save the Queen," in our honour; but it was played in such quick time that all the effects usually inspired by its martial strains were removed.

Once previously, at a small French theatre where "Round the World in Eighty Days" was being performed, I had heard our glorious anthem rattled through at a similar pace. On that occasion the typical Englishmen of Frenchmen (with due deference to Max O'Rell) invariably turned up in a well-developed dice-board suit of dittos, leading an unhappy bulldog very gingerly by a string. Though acting in French, this individual interlarded his lines with innumerable "damns," to the manifest delight of the audience. This was raised to a still higher pitch when, by a little gag and by-play, he expostulated with the "damn'd boule-dag," whom he thus anathematised for a pretended unwillingness at being hauled off the boards.

Upon the completion of the tour, and consequent winning of the wager, "God save the Queen" was played to the time of a rattling hand gallop, and its reproduction at Teneriffe in such quick time recalled this former experience to my memory.

The house was by no means a full one, and the prices of admission were very modest. A young Spanish girl was pointed out as the local heiress, and her boundless fortune spoken of in such glowing terms that crude ideas began to creep over one of the party that she might perhaps not be disinclined towards a son of the Emerald Isle. On inquiry, we ascertained that her dowry was equivalent to about twelve hundred pounds English, though it sounded quite a respectable sum in "reales," and our Irishman thought he had better, after all, stick to the "Houssa" constabulary.

Grand Canary was our next port of call. This island has a much more barren and rugged appearance than either Madeira or Teneriffe. Here, as at Teneriffe, innumerable vendors of cigars, canaries, and Florida water, board the ship and haggle over their wares. The prices rapidly declined as the hour of departure drew near, until at last passengers were importuned to make purchases at less than half the prices demanded in the first instance. Strange to say, the principal article imported into these islands is soap, and yet a dirtier or more unkempt lot than the Spaniards inhabiting them cannot be imagined, unless, in saying so, I do an injustice to the Portuguese at Madeira.

This was our last European port of call, and we were soon ploughing the wave, bound for that vast African continent which, despite all missionary attempts, is still steeped in heathenism and vice to its water's edge. The rapidly increasing heat inconveniently reminded us that we were well in the Torrid Zone.

The ship was covered with awning from stem to stern; but even this was insufficient protection from the sun; and solar topees had to be worn while on deck. Fortunately, there were no lady passengers, so we were allowed to revel in the luxury of pyjamas throughout the day, and these cool and comfortable coverings, together with shirts and turned-down collars, and the thinnest of ties, were by general consent adopted as mess-dress.

The part of the Atlantic through which the ship was passing is known to be one of the richest fishing-grounds in the world, and was for many years regularly visited by flotillas of fishing-smacks hailing from the Canaries. This industry has of late years been entirely neglected, owing to the extended field for trading opened up through the numerous steamers now calling at those islands for supplies.

CHAPTER III.

AN ADVENTURE AT SEA.

THE saloon of the "Senegal" occupied the whole of the space under the poop. The entrance to it on the main deck was by a narrow passage, in which the steward's pantry was also situated. One night, having dawdled longer than usual over our evening yarns and last pipe, we were interrupted by an extraordinary sound of rapidly approaching hoofs, and there was a general stampede for places of safety as a bullock rushed into the saloon, followed by a large Newfoundland dog, who appeared to consider this treat had been planned for his particular amusement, as he irritated the flanks of the beast.

The bullock seemed quite dazed by the novelty of his position, and the sudden change from the outer darkness to this inner chamber of light. After a slight pause, chased by the dog, he trotted to the end of the saloon, where one of the stewards whose duty it was to sleep in the saloon that night was lying on the settee extended across the stern of the vessel, worn out by the fatigues of the hot day.

The animal's wet nose, while trying to find a possible exit in this quarter, touched the steward's face, and partly aroused him from his slumbers; for, after one or two ineffectual pushes with his hands, and the usual stretches and yawns given by an awakening sleeper, one hand came in contact with the bullock's moist face.

"Oh, Holy Mother in heaven!—oh, glory!" What's the matter?" he ejaculated, and, rubbing his half-opened eyes, he perceived, in horrified amazement, a pair of horns, the liquid eyes, and the outlines of the black visage of the bullock, which, to his slowly awakening imagination, doubtless assumed a terribly realistic shape.

"Och! where am I a'thall? Is it meself that says (sees) it at last?—or is it draiming that I am?" he continued, as vainly and with stricken fear he doubted his own eyesight, and endeavoured to keep this horrible nightmare at arm's length.

With a blanched and pallid face that steward

now stood upright, his hair standing on end, beads of perspiration on his brow, while with an expression of agonised terror he shouted, "Help! help! Alf—Mr. Jones!—Come quick, some of yez; shure it's meself 'll be gored ef somebody don't pall the baste away,"—as now thoroughly awake he perceived the actual state of affairs, and then saw us passengers in the background convulsed with laughter.

"Shure, its helpin' me, and not laughin', yez ought to be," expostulated the steward.

"Take him by the head and turn him round," shouted the fat purser, personally in a safe position.

"Arrah, sir! don't be foolin' me wid the baste's horns agin me ribs," answered McLouglin, and again continued spasmodically, as the animal made an attempt to push past him. "Oh! for the love of mercy, take howld of his tail before I'm kilt entirely—think of the childer without"——: and then energetically, "Pull him off, I tell ye!—pull him off!—shure the dog's druv him mad, bad 'cess to him. Ah! now, ye wouldn't all of yez stand by and see a poor bhoy ripped up like a shape (sheep); would yez, now?"

Upon this we seized hold of the bullock's tail

as he had certainly become more demonstrative in the direction of the steward. After continued tuggings, we succeeded in making the brute turn round; but as this brought him face to face with us, we all beat a rapid and ignominous retreat, some being satisfied by getting the table between them and the animal, while others, less bold, dived under it as a safer refuge from danger.

Our fright had by now extended to the bullock, who again galloped down the saloon, only to stop in amazement opposite the large pier-glass over the buffet, at which he would have doubtless run but for his reflection, which must have appeared to the beast as another of his own species approaching.

"Oh, horr'd, it 'll be the mirror he'll be afther breaking now," shouted the steward, getting over his fright at the prospect of this new disaster.

Resolutely seizing hold of the animal's tail, he added, "Come on, all of yez, an' we'll pull him round agin, an' out of the dure back foremost."

Accordingly we laid hold once more of the brute's tail. After repeated tuggings, which were ineffectual, McLoughlin, who had again become the leading man, gave the tail an artistic twist, and then a bite. This brought the bullock round with such celerity that much damage was done to the handsome maple panelling. As the space between the table and the side of the saloon was too narrow to permit of our following the tail, the brute was again face to face with us, at uncomfortably close quarters. This was too much for our valour, so *sauve qui peut* was the cry, as we once more ignominiously sought places of safety in anything but decorous order; thus leaving the bullock master of the situation.

The animal at last became quite infuriated, and in his frantic endeavours to get round the saloon, he scrambled first on to the settee, and from that to the table, over which a handsome swinging tray, laden with its wealth of glass, extended the full length of the saloon. Catching his horns in this, the whole structure came down with a terrific crash, smashing the glass to atoms, bringing down the lamps with it, while the brute rolled off amidst the débris of broken .glass and splinters of wood, a large piece of the swinging tray remaining suspended from one of his horns, as an irritating but highly ludicrous trophy.

The uproar was now indescribable, and the wrecked appearance of the saloon gave unmistakeable proof of the destructive capabilities of the proverbial bull in a china-shop. Ultimately the creature charged straight for the door, scattering the few sailors who were clustered round, looking astonished at the unusual proceedings.

The captain, who had retired early in the evening, had not been present during any part of this scene, but the noise at length reached his ears. Thinking it was time for the passengers to desist from such uproarious conduct, he entered the saloon, evidently without the remotest knowledge of how the disaster had occurred.

After looking with astonishment at the wrecked state of affairs, he turned to the passengers, and in a very quiet tone, and with a serious face, he said: "Now, gentlemen, what's the meaning of this disgraceful conduct?"

We were all eager to explain, when he interrupted us. "Stop, gentlemen; let one speak at a time, please. Quartermaster, tell the first mate to come to me!" Then catching sight of the purser at the far end of the saloon ruefully regarding the remnants of an American organ which was his private property, he called out:

"Mr. Thurston, how did this happen?"

Mr. Thurston: "Why, sir, the bull—— oh, my poor harmonium!"

Captain: "Your poor harmonium! the bull! What bull, sir?"

Mr. Thurston: "Yes, sir, the bull we bought at Madeira."

Captain (roaring): "D——n the bull at Madeira. I want to know, sir, which of these gentlemen are to blame for this disgraceful conduct?"

Mr. Thurston, desperately, and speaking volubly, explained how the bull had done it, and all that had occurred.

The captain's seriousness had set us laughing again, and the study of his face as the storm-clouds slowly passed away, giving place first to a sunny smile, and then to a broad grin as the whole scene gradually dawned upon him, was so irresistibly comic, that he joined in the general hilarity, and peals of laughter were heard on all sides as he fully admitted that he had added an amusing sequel to the strange event.

The first officer, who had been keeping watch on the bridge, now entered and started back with surprise and dismay at the scene before him. This was redoubled when he saw us laughing until our sides were aching, amidst a scene of such confusion and destruction.

First officer: "Yessir?"

Captain: "I don't want you now, Bates, it's all over! Ha-ha-ha!"

Omnes: "Ha-ha-ha!"

Mr. Bates (looking very hard at the captain and the rest): "Yes, sir, so it seems: but in the name of Heaven, how—did—this—happen What's up?"

Captain (spasmodically): "Why, Bates,—the bull,—the harmonium,—and I,—oh!—the passengers."

Bates (in puzzled tones): "The bull! the harmonium! and you owe the passengers! Yessir."

"Oh, yes, I thought it was a row among the passengers; but it was the bull which got loose and found its way in here," said the captain as he rapidly detailed the circumstances, adding, "but come, gentlemen, let us have a drink?"

McLoughlin: "Ef yer plaise sorr, there's no tumblers, they're all broke, ivery one; but there's cups an' some mugs, if they'll do?"

We heard next day that the bullock, after leaving the saloon, had proceeded to the fo'castle, overturning one of the quartermasters in his flight, and succeeded in entering the sailors' cabin, where they had equal difficulty in expelling this unwelcome visitor.

The damage done to the saloon was estimated at over two hundred pounds, and yet the animal had not been twenty minutes in accomplishing his disastrous work. Inquiry showed that the bullock had chafed the halter with which he was fastened, until it had parted, and then found his way into the saloon, probably attracted by the light, with the amusing though costly results described.

By this time everyone had settled down in the groove of sea life; and chaff, badinage, and repartee, together with quaint and sad stories of African life, helped to pass away the idle time inseparable from a passenger's life on board ship. On the sixth day after leaving Madeira we arrived at Goree, the harbour of which is formed by the space between the small island on which the settlement stands, and the mainland of Africa, where the white houses of the town of Dakar lie along the sea-shore.

CHAPTER IV.

GOREE AND THE GAMBIA.

GOREE has obtained the unenviable distinction of being extremely unhealthy, even in this unhealthy portion of the earth's surface, and looking at the hot arid rock, capped by the antiquated fort, it can be easily imagined that its reputation has not been maligned. The rays of the sun beat pitilessly on this barren spot, unrelieved by the shadow of any friendly trees, until the air seems to dance with the germs of an atmospheric nebulæ most irritating to the eyes. Yellow fever is almost indigenous, and month after month, at oft-repeated intervals, the harbour is closed through the prevalence of this scourge. In this state of affairs it would be supposed that the French local authorities would not be over sensitive concerning the possibility of danger from a ship "outward bound."

But the oft-repeated expression that things are better managed under French rule, may explain the want of perception on my part in not grasping the object of the stringent inquiries demanded from the ship by the health officer, a most sickly-looking individual, who came alongside. After minutely inspecting the various health reports from the previous ports of call, he felt it was his duty to ask a few questions.

Health Officer: "Have you discovered any *sickyness* to your vessel since the last port you arrested?"

Captain: "No—none at all."

Health Officer: "Haive you any voyagers to this port?"

Captain: "Oh, yes, I have made several. What the ——"

Health Officer: "Pardong—you not comprehend. Is there to land from the ship any voyagers?"

Having received an answer to the effect that there were no passengers for Goree, the man in authority, after serious consultation with another "tricoloured" official (for it is as well to affect importance at times, to add to one's dignity), relunctantly granted us pratique.

The appearance of the island of Goree from the sea, though somewhat picturesque, was most uninviting; and travelling experience proves, that while distant prospects are often deceptive in suggesting beauty, which closer acquaintance does *not* confirm, it invariably follows that when a landscape does not appear harmonious at a distance, it will be found to be still more disappointing upon closer inspection. The scenery on the mainland, too, appeared tame and bare. For, though a stretch of desert, with one solitary palm, or better still, with a camel burying its head in the sand, is charmingly artistic on canvas, it is not from want of appreciation of "things beautiful," that I express the decided opinion that the picture has much the best of it.

However, by raising the curiosity of a youthful fellow passenger eager to get an early glimpse of African life, I was enabled to obtain a companion to accompany me on shore. So, engaging a boatman, who deftly lowered the sail and brought his large craft alongside the pier just as it seemed inevitable that we should be dashed against it, we braved the sweltering heat and landed at Goree.

We visited the fort and one or two of the

public buildings, and then entered the market-place. Here a crowd of miserable women were making a babel of sounds in their hagglings over their paltry wares. Squatting in all manner of positions before their baskets were old and grizzly-haired negresses, their bodies covered with ulcerous sores; their eyes almost destroyed by ophthalmic diseases, exuding gangrenous matter upon which flies settled apparently unmolested; while the repulsive appearance of their nude emaciated forms, shrunken shanks and maimed figures, combined with the nauseating smell to force us, choking, away from a scene of squalor and wretchedness encountered for the first time.

The political history of Goree has been a very chequered one, it having changed hands no fewer than twelve times in the last two centuries. Originally ceded to the Dutch in 1617 by a native potentate, it was captured by the English, only to be retaken by the Dutch, from whom it was arrested by the French in 1677, when it shortly afterwards again fell into English hands. It was subsequently restored to the French by treaty, but since then, in the numerous wars between England and France, it has changed hands no fewer than six times, only to be recaptured or restored.

As a trading emporium and coaling station, it is doubtless valuable, and in the distant future may be of still greater importance. But, like the rest of the stations on the West Coast of Africa, its pestilential climate surrounds its possession with a deep margin of mourning for the loss of those officers who die in the service of their country, unattended by the excitement or glory of war.

The next port, Bathurst, a British possession, is situated on a small sand-bank, dignified by the name of St. Mary's Island, some twelve miles up the majestic Gambia River. This river, until a comparatively recent date, was erroneously believed to be an affluent of the mighty Niger. It has now been found to have a separate source, though so close to that of the Niger as to justify the early opinion that they were connected. The Gambia is navigable for vessels of light draught for several hundreds of miles. Vast ideas were entertained of the unknown resources believed to be lying idle on its banks, and of the importance of some of the native towns in its vicinity. Its possession was, therefore, regarded as the key to a large interior trade, which might, at an early date, be available to the outer world.

With a view of obtaining reliable information on the future prospects of this river, and with the object of developing the trade already existing, a Government expedition recently started, and going by boat as far as a small town called "Bady," proceeded thence inland to "Timbo," the capital of the "Futah Jallon" country. This town was believed to contain many thousands of inhabitants, to be rich in gold and precious stones, and to be the emporium of a considerable interior trade. So fabulous were the stories of the wealth of this district, that the construction of a railway to "Timbo" was considered a practicable financial operation.

The expedition scattered all hopes of this African Golconda to the winds; the country *en route* was found to be so sparsely populated, that Governor Gouldsbury, in describing his journey by river, refers to the solitude of the voyage in the following descriptive words:—
"From the summit of some hills whose headlands abutted on the river, an extensive view was obtained of the surrounding country, which

as a rule is flat, and uninteresting, and supposed to be quite uninhabited. Indeed, the eye searched in vain for homestead or hamlet, for clearing or cultivation or other sign of human occupancy of the land, but met instead, with the sadness of—what it is no hyperbole to call—the 'abomination of desolation' which reigned over the scene. Not a single canoe or other vessel was seen throughout the whole length of the river from Yarbutenda to the wharf at Bady—a distance of some one hundred and eighty miles; and from the date of Governor McDonnel's expedition in 1849 until we appeared—a lapse of thirty-two years,—its surface bore no other burden than the floating leaf, the broken branch, and the fallen tree."

The few villages through which the expedition passed were small, and produced nothing for exportation, while the tribes inhabiting them were engaged in the usual cruel internecine wars which seem to be an essential condition of African existence. When "Timbo" itself was reached, it was found to contain less than two thousand inhabitants, and these split up into various small townships, in order to facilitate defence. The amount of grain grown was insufficient for the wants of the inhabitants, and the expeditionary force had much difficulty in renewing the supplies for the native carriers. No gold, or precious stones, were known to exist in the vicinity, and there was little hope of "Timbo" ever becoming the source of any considerable trade.

All manual labour in the Gambia settlement is performed by women, and numbers of them were engaged in loading lighters, with infants straddled on their backs. About a hundred of them were engaged in unloading a barge filled with cargo from our ship, under the superintendence of a native overseer. This man evidently thought our presence an excellent opportunity of airing his importance, for he poured upon the women labourers an incessant vocabulary of abuse, which ultimately so enraged them that they went to him *en masse*, and with such violent intentions that he fled up the street precipitately, pursued and pelted by them. The women then quietly returned and proceeded with their work, but the overseer, deeming discretion the better part of valour, did not again put in an appearance.

Owing to the quantity of cargo for this

station, and the absence of any systematic arrangement for landing it, each consignee arranging for himself, the "Senegal" was to stay here over two days. These would have been most monotonous days indeed, but for the appearance of a shark. To obtain a hook from the chief officer, and bait it with pork, was the work of a few minutes, and we soon had eight or ten of them fighting over the coveted morsel. We hooked five, and they gave great sport as they rushed madly about in their frantic endeavours to get free. On almost every occasion we had them fast on, and played them until exhausted, but whenever we attempted to haul one on board, it unaccountably ended in the brute getting away.

One of the mates afterwards explained that it is almost impossible to land a shark in this way, since the jaws are not sufficiently strong to hold the immense weight of the body. In order to haul one on deck, a noose, or running bowline with a hitch, should be passed over the hook-line. The shark, being played on top of the water, would wriggle itself into the hitch, which should be tightened when below the dorsal fin. Had we known this, we should certainly have secured several, as we frequently had them well hooked, and played them until they were tired.

Nothing could be more fiendish than the fierce expression of hatred that gleamed from the eyes of these brutes, as they lashed the water into foam in their frantic endeavours to get free. One that I peppered with swan-shot while held on the surface of the water, sprang clean out of it several times in its maddened attempts, ultimately snapping the thick line (a new signal halyard), as though it were pack-thread, and made off with the hook firmly secured in its jaws.

Sharks are well known to possess an extraordinary amount of vitality. I once planted several Snider·bullets in a shark which had been left in a small lagoon at shoal tide, without succeeding in doing it much apparent harm. A shark's heart will pulsate for many hours, if placed in a bucket of warm water; and I have been told by an authority whom I have no reason to doubt, that if a shark be disembowelled, the rest of the body, if returned to the sea, will mechanically go through the motions of swimming for a short while.

Those playing round the "Senegal" were probably of one species, though they differed considerably in colour and size. Some of them were of a dull leaden hue with a lighter shade on the belly, while others were beautifully marked in stripes, in a manner resembling the coarser mackerel more than any other fish I can call to mind. I was told that these were tiger sharks, and supposed to be specially savage. But as I noticed a variety of changing colours in others, I am more inclined to think that their marking is influenced by the feeding-ground which they frequent, those of a dull-grey hue having been, probably, for a long time denizens of the muddy river, thereby losing the brighter rainbow colours of the others, that had but recently come in from deep-sea soundings. This is surely a provision of nature, as otherwise they would have great difficulty in securing their prey?

With regard to the fierceness of the different species of these brutes, while I do not pretend to speak with equal authority to many writers, I doubt if any can exceed in ferocity the small ordinary grey shark, seldom seen above ten feet long, and which rarely shows itself on the surface of the water, except to seize its unfortunate victim, with which it will fight with the greatest fury.

St. Mary's Island, on which the settlement now stands, is divided from the mainland by a narrow channel, dignified by the name of Oyster Creek, and the trade with the interior has to be conducted by the aid of barges and canoes. Numerous attempts to bridge over this narrow ferry have failed, owing to an amount of blundering which would have been fatal to the reputation of the merest tyro in engineering in any other part of the world. These repeated failures would be laughable were they not so injurious to the trade of the station; nor can they impress the natives with a very exalted idea of British engineering skill.

On one occasion it really appeared as though the bridge was within measurable distance of completion, and with great pride a few of the piles were pointed out as they stood proudly erect above the stream. The inevitable congratulatory addresses were in course of preparation, in which due weight was laid upon the completion of this "missing link" to unite St. Mary's Island to the vast mainland. But some ingenious native fishermen had the temerity to fasten their canoe to one of these piles, while they followed their dangerous and precarious calling.

Alas! the strain of the light "dug out" was too much for the stability of the upright post, for it toppled over, unfortunately sinking the canoe, and resulting in the death by drowning of the unhappy crew. The coroner sat upon their remains, and the jury returned a verdict of "Accidental death": but history does not record whether they referred to the rashness of the fishermen in thus risking their lives. The remaining piles, probably from shame, gradually bowed in the direction of the running stream, until they also passed calmly on, and were washed ashore lower down the river.

On another occasion the piles were ordered out from England, and duly arrived in all the highly-finished elegance of British workmanship. By some strange fatality they were all the same length; by another coincidence, the soundings had apparently been taken at low tide, and no allowance made for such an unusual daily occurrence as high water. Consequently these piles still grace the side of the beach in a horizontal and useless position, while another local engineer was sent up from Sierra Leone to inspect them, and to add a farther report on the mighty subject. The bridge is to this day talked of, and there is little doubt that its construction is still in course of energetic progress, on foolscap paper. Should it ever be finished, a statement of its absolute cost, inclusive of false starts, will be a matter of interest, stamping it as one of the most expensive structures of the kind ever completed.

The Portuguese first settled in the Gambia River in the fifteenth century, and it became a bone of contention between England and France at different periods of its early history. The first British settlement was on James' Island, a very small sandbank some thirty-five miles from the river's mouth. In 1817 the river was finally recognised as a British possession by the Treaty of Paris, and the site of the settlement was then moved to the present Island of St. Mary's, which is larger, strategically better, and more healthy than James' Island. But, notwithstanding the Treaty of Paris, the possession of the Gambia was much coveted by the French, who hampered the English trade by starting a settlement just below Bathurst, on the mainland, at a place called Albrada, which has since been surrendered.

Even within the last few years, energetic overtures for an exchange of the Gambia for some other river in Africa (probably the Gaboon, now possessed by the French), have been made, and it is supposed that nothing but the timely protest of the natives and merchants of the settlement prevented the exchange being effected. With the possession of this river, the French would soon obtain an uninterrupted stretch of territory from Goree to Mellaevierie, or Binty, which are in proximity to Sierra Leone. If the Gambia were ever ceded to them, the annexation of the intermediate country between the points above mentioned would soon follow, and the immense seaboard and rivers comprised in that area would inevitably become French property.

Besides St. Mary's, small outstations are maintained at several points higher up the Gambia River. The principal of these is situated about one hundred and fifty miles from the river's mouth on McCarthy's Island—so called in memory of the popular governor of that name under whose able supervision the whole of the British possessions on the West Coast made their first step in prosperity and advancement. The heat in these up-stations is intense, as they do not receive the benefit of the sea breezes; consequently residence in them is particularly fatal to white people. But since they may some day be of importance to the river trade, a contingent of native police now represents law, and maintains a crude link of civilization with the outer world.

A mail every three weeks outward-bound calls at the Gambia, and homeward-bound steamers call once a fortnight. Although financially and departmentally separated from Sierra Leone, it is under the authority of the Governor of that colony, who in consequence enjoys the distinguished title of Governor-in-Chief of the West Africa Settlements. In the first instance this high-sounding title covered the whole of Her Majesty's possessions on the West Coast, from the Gambia to the Gold Coast, and Lieutenant Governors were established under his authority at the different stations. His residence was at Sierra Leone, and a steamer called the "Sherb'ro," officered from the navy, was maintained, so as to enable the Governor-in-Chief to visit the various seats of his authority. This arrangement was, however, altered, and the Gold Coast was by royal charter lopped off and made a distinct appointment; but in virtue of his continued authority over the Gambia the original title still remains.

The Gambia trade of the present day consists almost exclusively in the exportation of ground nuts, from which much of the "olive oil" of modern times is extracted, and the importation of cotton stuffs, trade guns, gunpowder, African finery, and the vilest of trade spirits. The principal tribes near the settlement belong to the Jollof and Foulah race. They possess the comely features and lithe stature of the Arab, while their religion is a mixture of Mohammedanism and Paganism, in which Fetishism and Superstition play cruel and degrading parts.

CHAPTER V.

NATIVE PECULIARITIES, AND A TORNADO.

ABOUT a hundred deck passengers joined the ship, bound for different parts of the coast, to trade. Of these, by far the greater number were women. These were nearly all mothers, and I was much interested in the manner in which one of them supplied her infant with a small amount of artificial nutriment. Taking an empty condensed milk tin, she placed in it a small quantity of the milk from another tin, and, after adding a plentiful supply of water, she churned it up with her finger. Then, placing her hand under the child's chin, in the form of a hollow, she poured some of the milk into it. As the wretched infant's mouth was covered with milk, there was no other alternative but to swallow or choke, and for some time I thought it would do the latter. The baby, I suppose, was used to it, for although the operation was continued again and again, it managed to survive, and after the mother considered sufficient had been administered, it went off to sleep, evidently none the worse for its " swallow or die " meal.

The women appear to be most affectionate mothers, and as they toil at their work in the fields, or carry huge baskets through the streets, vending their wares, they talk cheerfully to the little black ball, whose woolly head may be seen peeping out of the capacious shawl by which it is straddled on the mother's back, and from this safe position it coos back prattling answers to the mother's endearing remarks. Such scenes could not but forcibly recall to my mind that, but a few years back, mothers and children were ruthlessly torn apart; while those who supported such inhumanity boldly asserted that these people were devoid of such feelings for their young as even the brute creation possess.

The head-dresses worn by the women consisted of handkerchiefs tied in a pyramidical fashion peculiar to the Jollofs, who also do their hair in a mass of tiny plaits, generally reeking of powerfully-scented oils. After a short residence on the coast, it is easily seen that the women of the different tribes adopt distinct methods of arranging their hair and tying their handkerchiefs on it, and would never dream of copying that of another tribe. Such habits, together with marked characteristics, in dress and features, of both sexes, enable the student interested in racial peculiarities to distinguish the various tribes: for the negro, like the Caucasian, is divided into many subdivisions, whose separate origin may, in the no-distant future, afford interesting opportunities of historical research.

A native dandy also came on board as a first-class passenger bound for Sierra Leone. This fact was notified for general information by the printed labels pasted over his numerous trunks (all of modest dimensions and dubious quality), and it was made still more apparent by the very large type of the placards which set forth:

With Care.	*With Care.*
W. E. GLADSTONE-BARNES, Esq., b.a.,	
FOURAH BAY COLLEDGE,	
SIERRA LEONE.	
CHIEF SALOON PASSENGER.	
N.B.—Wanted through the Voyage.	

As Sierra Leone is the next port of call after the Gambia, and but forty-eight hours' journey, this amount of ostentation was truly appalling, though it probably had the desired effect of magnifying the importance of the journey—and the individual—in the eyes of his many sable friends who came to see him off. They bade him a most demonstrative farewell, and their frequent use of such familiar phrases as " Write soon, old fellow," " Good-bye, dear chappie," and " By jove, sah," showed the inevitable bump of imitative faculty which, among the negroes, may be truly said to amount to an absolute talent.

The captain looked askance at all the belongings, which were, " N.B. Wanted through the voyage ; " but Mr. G.-B. was so importunate, and begged so hard that they might be left handy, that they were at last permitted to remain on the top of the hatchway, which was again battened down, as we slowly steamed out of the river.

Just before dinner was served in the evening, the following conversation occurred between the chief steward and the purser:

Chief Steward : " If you please, sir, into which cabin am I to put the new coloured gentleman ? "

Purser: "Oh, with the other coloured gentleman."

The captain, at the other end of the table, then explained to us, in a low voice, that Africans much dislike being referred to as either "negroes," or even "black gentlemen," while the term "nigger" is looked upon as such an absolute insult that natives have been known to take out an action and obtain damages against anyone using it. The stewards, with a keen regard to their perquisites, rarely forget to indulge this somewhat harmless weakness.

Shortly after leaving the Gambia, the sky in the distance over the low receding land became inky black, while the lightning flashed intermittently and vividly, followed by long, deep, rolling, clashing thunder. And yet the night was fine: overhead and out towards the ocean the stars were shining brightly in the glow of a calm evening, while the moon cast her silvery sheeny light over the quiet sea.

The black clouds rapidly approached towards the sea. The captain's experience at once foretold a tornado, and quiet seaman-like orders were given to make all tight, so as to weather the coming blast. The darkness soon encompassed the vessel, and the outline of the lowering clouds assumed the shape of a clearly-cut arc, driving before it, at incredible speed, a rolling grey mist, forming a lighter veil to the inky black ground. The gentle breeze which had been blowing gave place to a lull of short duration, followed by a few preparatory soughs; a few warning drops of rain; and the tornado burst upon us, lashing the sea into a seething foam, the wind whistling through the cordage with a weird tempestuous sound, as the gallant "Senegal" struggled in the hurricane.

The rain descended in torrents, the furious wind, the brilliant lightning—in which the inky darkness can only be described as intervening, and the crashing thunder, all combined to create a feeling of wondrous awe, and I stood enchained on deck, regardless of the storm, a fascinated spectator of this war between earth and heaven.

> Black grew the sky—all black, all black;
> The clouds were everywhere;
> There was a feeling of suspense
> In nature, a mysterious sense
> Of terror in the air.

> Eight bells! and suddenly abaft,
>   With a great rush of rain,
> Making the ocean white with spume;
>   In darkness like the day of doom,
>   On came the hurricane.
>
> The lightning flashed from cloud to cloud,
>   And rent the sky in two;
> A jagged flame, a single jet
>   Of white fire, like a bayonet,
>   That pierced the eyeballs through.
>   —*Longfellow's* "*The Ballad of Carmelham.*"

In about half an hour the tornado had spent itself, and our course again lay through calm seas, and under moonlit sky, while the air seemed to be relieved of the oppressive sultriness which had preceded the storm.

The tornado seasons occur twice in the year, preceding and following upon the "rains." The duration of each of these seasons is about six weeks. They begin somewhat irregularly, and then increase in severity and regularity until they are of daily occurrence, when they gradually die away. A tornado invariably bursts at low or high water, and the peculiar appearance of the sky always affords timely notice of its approach. In the rivers, the natives know exactly how long they can with safety carry sail on their boats, and when to seek shelter, or to lower sail and prepare to face the coming

NATIVE PECULIARITIES, AND A TORNADO. 51

blast, which carries their crafts many miles down the river.

Next morning, Mr. Barnes' boxes showed unmistakeable traces of the effects of their exposure to the heavy rain, the place where they were piled being under the open lashings of the awning. The contents were mixed up in a general pulp, which augured badly for the dash he had been hoping to cut upon landing at Sierra Leone. While he was ruefully regarding a pair of shapeless inexpressibles, hanging damp and sodden from his uplifted hands, and which, from his lamentations, must have been exceptional favourites, the captain came up. With an expression of face in which pretended commiseration struggled vainly with a desire to laugh, he asked: "What! wanted already through the voyage?"

Sierra Leone was sighted in good time next day, and long before the ship anchored the sun had dried Mr. Barnes' belongings; but it could not restore them to their original satisfactory shape.

Freetown, the capital of the settlement, lies at the foot of the lofty ridge of hills from the configuration of which the place derives its name

(Ridge of Lions). The town is built along the shore about four miles from the mouth of the magnificent estuary formed by the confluence of the Sierra Leone and Rokelle Rivers, with their numerous minor tributaries. The mouth of the estuary is protected by a sandbank extending nearly across the harbour, leaving, however, a perfectly safe channel of sufficient width near the Lighthouse Point.

Passing slowly up to the anchorage, one is struck with the extreme beauty of the surrounding country. On the right-hand side innumerable small bays open out abruptly in diversified form, now leading to a gently ascending hill, now, varied by bold crag and jutting headland, while the thick bush and the massive silk cotton trees, with their curiously twisted trunks, form a background frequently relieved by patches of rude cultivation on which farm houses and negro villages are picturesquely situated. The low Bullom shore on the opposite side of the estuary with its stretch of sandy beach, improves the effect produced by the rugged volcanic edge before us.

To the left of the town, which is situated on a promontory, the winding river is seen,

NATIVE PECULIARITIES, AND A TORNADO. 53

its broad expanse dotted with numerous islets covered with the pliant ligneous mangrove plant, on whose interlaced roots oysters cluster in profusion, while the dense bush affords a safe retreat to the monkey, the crocodile, and birds of brilliant plumage.

Directly the ship received pratique, she was boarded by a swarm of negroes of both sexes, bent upon buying or selling, which was carried on with much laughter and noisy haggling. Almost every sailor and steward belonging to either of the two lines of steamers dividing the West African trade, brings out goods for trade. These are gradually exposed for sale as the ships approach the coast, until the fo'castle assumes the appearance of a Cheap-Jack bazaar, in which knives, boots, pipes, toys, looking-glasses, hats, jams, pictures, ribbons, ladies' stays, and men's continuations are mixed up in picturesque confusion.

It is by no means an uncommon thing to see a weather-beaten quartermaster, with tarred hands, engaged in selling a gorgeously-trimmed hat to a negress, who, planting it on top of her handkerchief-bound head, admiringly surveys the effect in a sixpenny mirror, also an article of commerce; while the son of Neptune, with arms akimbo, assures her that she "looks a reg'lar booty," and that "the 'at is a rare bargain for seven-and-six."

This floating retail business has gradually arisen owing to the innumerable ports these vessels call at on the voyage; and by this means the natives are able to obtain many useful things they would otherwise have much difficulty in procuring. Occasional endeavours have been made by the companies to stop the traffic, owing to the complaints of the local traders, who consider that it injures their business. But when rigorous prohibition was enforced, the companies found considerable difficulty in obtaining the same steady class of seamen. At present they wisely content themselves with carefully overhauling the sailor's belongings before they start on the voyage; but "Jack" is quite cunning enough to find means of evading this search, and the inevitable bazaar is always started when once the ship arrives on the coast.

It was now my turn to say good-bye to fellow passengers and officers, with whom I had passed such an agreeable voyage, and, as the government boat, pulled by Kroo boys, was conveying me to the shore, little did I think that the fair-haired lad bound to the Gold Coast, who had been my special chum at sea, and who was gaily waving a parting farewell from the bridge, would succumb to the virulent coast fever ere the "Senegal" made her homeward-bound call at Sierra Leone, less than two months afterwards.

CHAPTER VI.

EARLY HISTORY OF THE SETTLEMENT.

In 1772, through the noble exertions of Granville Sharp, the pioneer of negro emancipation, Lord Mansfield pronounced his famous legal decision, declaring Slavery unlawful in Great Britain. In consequence of this decision, in a few months numbers of negroes, who were in England with their owners, received their liberty. They were living in beggary, unable to obtain work, and mainly supported by the charitable assistance of the few philanthropists who had previously taken up their cause.

As these freed slaves increased in numbers it became a matter of serious importance, and one even receiving Government consideration, that means should be found for providing for their necessities. To send them to any British colony would be sending them back to a condition of slavery, since slavery was still lawful in our colonial possessions. It was equally impossible that they could continue living, either on charity, charitable subscribers, or in idle beggary ; while public opinion was for some time, not unfavourable to the owners, who considered Lord Mansfield's judgment a direct interference with a portion of their goods and chattels, for which they had paid the market price.

Ultimately the idea occurred to Granville Sharp to send these liberated slaves to the coast of Africa, through the aid of charitable subscribers, and with them form a settlement, where they might not only live in freedom and earn their own livelihood, but also be the means of benefiting the natives, and introducing Christianity among them.

With this object in view, a "Committee for the Relief of the Black Poor" was formed, and it was suggested by one of the members that Sierra Leone would be a suitable place at which to start this new venture. The Government readily co-operated in the arrangements, and placed a vessel at the disposal of the Committee. After certain unavoidable delays, several hundreds of Africans and a few white volunteers, under the charge of an "Agent Conductor" sailed for the West Coast of Africa, and landed at Sierra Leone in August, 1787—A CENTURY AGO.

A small plot of land, situated about six miles from the mouth of the estuary, was purchased from a native chief, and the settlers began their up-hill work of founding the first Free African Colony.

Unfortunately, but little thought had been given to the pestilential nature of the climate, and the settlers, who had previously fallen into vicious habits in England, were ill fitted for the arduous trials before them. The rainy season was at its height when they landed, and as a consequence, in a few months, sickness and death made sad havoc in the little band. The "Agent Conductor" and several of his assistants were among the first to fall victims to the dreaded malarial fever, while those who were fortunate enough to recover became dispirited and disheartened, as they suffered again and again from the effects of this enervating climate.

But the deadly coast fever was by no means the only calamity threatening the existence of the colony, for, within two years of landing, the town raised under such disadvantageous circumstances was plundered and destroyed by a native chief and his followers, and the settlers driven to take shelter in the mountains.

However, in England the able band of reformers had been most energetic in the cause of Freedom. An association was established, called "The St. George's Bay Company," which acquired increased powers from the Crown for the extension of the colony. With this Company "the Committee for the relief of the Black Poor" soon merged, and the combined directors obtained, in 1789, a Royal Charter. Assistance was promptly despatched to the dispirited settlers, whose sinking hopes were revived. A town was built on a new site, and called Granville Town, in honour of the man who first made the subject of negro liberation the work of his life.

The St. George's Bay Company gave way, in 1791, to the "Sierra Leone Company, which received extended privileges from the Crown. The objects of this Company were to establish the settlement, not only for philanthropic purposes, but as a commercial venture, and visionary hopes were entertained that what was being done in India could likewise be accomplished in Africa.

But the limited extent of territory over which any firm jurisdiction could be maintained, the sparseness of population, together with the extreme unhealthiness of the climate, which made adequate European supervision an impossibility, prevented the scheme becoming a financial success. Still, at home the question of Emancipation was being gradually pushed forward, and resulted in the settlement ultimately becoming of the greatest value when the abolition of slavery was finally determined upon.

During the war of American Independence large numbers of slaves were attracted to the side of the British by promises of pay, loot, and freedom. On the conclusion of hostilities, these negroes had been disbanded at Nova Scotia, and in the West Indies, and small grants of land were made to them by the Government. But as slavery was still in force, the planters strongly objected to these free natives, while the natives themselves were more inclined to lead a licentious idle life than turn to husbandry. Their liberty was of little use to them, since the colonists declined dealing with them or giving them work as free men, and their position became one of embarrassment to the Government.

The Sierra Leone Company offered to provide them with allotments at Sierra Leone, and the Government gladly agreed to the proposal. Accordingly, thirteen hundred of them were embarked for the West Coast, and arrived at Sierra Leone in the year 1792. As Granville Town was not sufficiently large to accommodate this great increase of population, the present site of Freetown, which is on a promontory facing the mouth of the estuary, was selected, and has since maintained its position as the capital of the settlement.

The original settlers had not been free from personal dissensions and quarrels, and this accession of turbulent spirits soon resulted in much mutinous conduct. This was secretly encouraged by the owners of the slave factories still carrying on their nefarious calling in close proximity to the colony, and they looked with dissatisfaction upon this endeavour to start a Free Settlement at the seat of their trade. To suppress these revolts, occasional assistance had to be sent from the English garrisons which were for the time being in possession of the Gambia and Goree.

But these local affrays, though serious in themselves, were completely overshadowed by a disaster unparalleled in the history of the colony. In 1794 a French squadron, under false colours, entered the harbour, and without warning opened fire on the defenceless settlement. In a few days the place was a heap of smouldering ruins, while a landing party pillaged and sacked the place, ruthlessly destroying all that they could not carry away. The vessels belonging to the company, lying in the harbour, were plundered and sunk; and desolation, ruin, and apparent starvation stared the luckless settlers in the face. Nor did the French stop here, for, having unfortunately gathered information of the expected arrival of two vessels from England, containing stores and provisions, they waited in the offing and captured both, adding them to the French fleet, which then sailed away.

However, before leaving, upon the earnest solicitation of the Governor, the French commander landed a few stores, and upon these, and the small amount of provisions which were overlooked in the relentless pillage, the colonists eked out a precarious existence until fresh supplies from home made their welcome appearance.

Before the commencement of hostilities between England and France (1st Feb., 1793), the objects of the settlement, as a purely philanthropic venture, had been explained to the French Republic, which agreed to look upon it as neutral, and even expressed approval of the undertaking. This fell blow, therefore, was as unexpected as it was unfair; for the English, relying on the good faith of the French, had left the place unprotected.

With that energy and devotion which had characterised all the actions of the directors from the beginning, they were not disheartened by this, but immediately set about restoring the town, and restarting the colony upon a firmer basis. Fresh stores were promptly forwarded to the distressed settlers, and the town rebuilt upon its ashes.

Such heavy financial strains very much interfered with the local progress of the settlers; and as disturbances again and again arose among them, the directors were frequently compelled to appeal to the Government for assistance and support. Consequently, in 1800 an additional Charter was granted, which created the settlement into an independent colony, with power to make laws for its good government. But before the extended privileges granted by this Charter arrived on the coast, the Nova Scotian settlers, aided by the Maroons, many of whom had also been brought over from the West Indies, broke out into open rebellion, and order was only restored after a sharp fight. The ringleaders were rightly made an example of, while the other malcontents were banished to the Bullom shore—a low marshy spot on the left bank of the estuary, from which they were not allowed to return to the settlement proper for several years.

In 1801-1802 the colony was twice invaded by the natives, who could not resist the temptation for plunder, but they were on each occasion repulsed with heavy loss. Notwithstanding these frequent disasters, local improvements were made. Freetown had been built upon a regular plan, the streets running in parallel lines; stores, churches, and schools were erected, and the negroes having at length become acclimatized, a gradual increase in trade and agriculture began to show itself.

FAVOURITE JOLLOF WIFE AND CHILD

But, as the expenses of the settlement increased with the rapid accession of imported population, without any return being sent home for the capital sunk in the enterprise, the affairs of the company became hopelessly embarrassed. This was increased by the withdrawal of the annual grants, hitherto paid by the Government, who had strong opinions that the colony had been mismanaged; and after a struggle of twenty years, during which the directors had to cope with many vicissitudes and expenses, grave thoughts were entertained of withdrawing from the venture, and abandoning the settlement.

The dissatisfaction of the Government with the management of the affairs of the settlement led to a parliamentary inquiry, and the Committee, in their report, strongly urged upon the Government the advisability of Sierra Leone being taken over by the Crown, adducing as one of the reasons, that the Crown would be better able to continue the work for which the settlement had been established. This suggestion was approved of; a bill for the purpose passed both Houses, and received His Majesty King George III.'s assent on the 8th August, 1807.

On the 1st January, 1808, a royal salute was fired from the Government House Battery, the Company's flag was hauled down, the Union Jack run up, and Sierra Leone embarked upon its new career as a Colony of the Crown.

CHAPTER VII.

SIERRA LEONE UNDER THE CROWN.

THOSE noble-minded men who had been instrumental in founding Sierra Leone still continued their crusade against the Slave Trade. Through their exertions a bill for its abolition was carried through Parliament, despite the efforts of many powerful opponents.

This act received the King's assent on the 25th March, 1807, and was to take effect from the 1st January, 1808. Hence, on the same date that the colony was formally handed over to the Crown, the Crown was bound by law to wage war against the continuance of the trade in human flesh.

It must not be understood, however, that the act above referred to abolished Slavery in our colonies, for it did not do so. It simply made the carrying of slaves beyond the seas unlawful.

So that, for many years (1808—1835), the curious anomaly existed of its being illegal to supply from one Crown colony the demand of a legally protected serfdom existing in another.

In order to provide for the maintenance of the slaves liberated by His Majesty's vessels on the West Coast of Africa, commodious barracks were built at Sierra Leone, and as heavy premiums stimulated the exertions of the officers and men engaged in suppressing the traffic, they were not long in making many captures. As cargo after cargo arrived at Sierra Leone, they were drafted to these establishments, where they received every attention and care until they recovered from the effects of the illtreatment and close and cruel confinement to which they had been subjected on board the slave vessels.

The condition of these wretched slaves as they were landed almost passes comprehension, and the harrowing scenes enacted as each slave-ship was purged of her living—ay, and her dead—freight, create feelings of astonishment that, but a few years since, there were men who openly championed the continuance of this disgraceful and inhuman traffic.

Mr. Rankin, in his visit to Sierra Leone, thus describes the condition of one of these captured slavers:—

"A painful interest prompted me to visit, as soon as possible, this prison ship. A friend offered the advantage of his company to a scene which has sometimes so completely overwhelmed a novice as to render the support of a friend advantageous.

"The Timmanee crew of the official boat swiftly shot us alongside. The craft showed Spanish colours, and was named "La Pantica." We easily leaped on board, as she lay low in the water. The first hasty glance around caused a sudden sickness and faintness, followed by an indignation more intense than discreet. Before us, lying in a heap, huddled together at the foot of the foremast, on the bare and filthy deck, lay several human beings in the last stage of emaciation—dying.

"The ship, fore and aft, was thronged with men, women, and children, all entirely naked, and disgusting with diseases. The stench was nearly insupportable—cleanliness being impossible. I stepped to the hatchway: it was secured by iron bars and cross-bars, and pressed against them were the heads of slaves below. It appeared that the crowd on deck formed one-third only of the cargo, two-thirds being stowed in a sitting posture below, between decks—the men forward, the women aft. Two hundred and seventy-four were at this moment in the little schooner. When captured, three hundred and fifteen had been found on board; forty had died during the voyage from Old Calabar, where she had been captured by His Majesty's ship, "Fair Rosamond." . . . . . . I attempted to descend, in order to see the accommodation. The height between the floor and the ceiling was about *twenty-two inches*. The agony of the position of the crouching slaves may be imagined, especially that of the men whose heads and necks are bent down by the boarding above them. Once so fixed, relief by motion or change of posture is unattainable. The body frequently stiffens into a premature curve; and in the streets of Freetown I have seen liberated slaves in every conceivable state of distortion."

Another such scene is depicted by a correspondent to a small local newspaper, and I am indebted to the late editor for kindly allowing me to copy the extract.

"Through the politeness of the prize officer, I was permitted to inspect the vessel. Although I had frequently been on board full slavers, on their arrival at this port, I certainly never was on board one where human beings were stowed in the smallest imaginable space, as was the case in this vessel. Five hundred and forty-seven human beings, besides the crew and passengers, twenty-eight in number, in a vessel of about ninety tons. The slaves were all stowed together, perfectly naked, with nothing but the surfaces of the water casks, which were made level by filling in billets of wood, which formed the slave deck.

"The slaves, who were confined in the hold—it being utterly impossible for the whole of them to remain on deck at one time,—were in a profuse state of perspiration, and panting like so many hounds for air and water. . . . . . I was informed that on the officers of the "Cygnet" boarding the slaver, the greater part of the slaves were chained together with pieces of chain, which were passed through iron collars round their necks, and shackles were also secured round their legs and arms. . . . . . They were branded like sheep. Letters were burnt in their skin of two inches in length. Many of them, from the recent period at which it had been done, were in a state of ulceration."

Reader, it must not be forgotten that these are descriptions of slavers which had been captured several weeks earlier than the times at which they were visited by the writers. During that interval the wretched beings had received better food, more water, and humane treatment as far as the limited spaces of the crowded vessels would permit it. What, then, must have been the condition of these human beings at the time of capture? Surely, I can answer without any exaggeration, a condition of heartrending misery, of agony, and of tortured pain, impossible to imagine, impossible to describe.

As an instance of the mortality that frequently occurred, even after capture by His Majesty's vessels, the slavery commissioners at Sierra Leone, in reporting upon the condition of the slaver "St. Helena," brought into Freetown to be condemned, stated that "one hundred and twenty, out of a total of five hundred and forty-nine slaves, died between the capture and the condemnation of the vessel" (a period of a few weeks. In some cases, half the living freight succumbed to the privations they had undergone between the time of the capture of the vessel and her arrival in port, and the African slave trade, in its mortality, must be stamped as a deadly trade, conducted with such gross inhumanity as, happily, to expedite its suppression.

One of the first Crown Governors was Sir Charles MacCarthy, and under his able direction arrangements were made for the care of the batches of slaves constantly arriving at the liberated African establishments. As these were released, many of them were indentured for a number of years as agricultural labourers, others found work under Government, in extending and repairing the roads, while some obtained admission into the African corps then existing.

But in order to provide accommodation for the rapidly increasing population, it became necessary to extend the limits of the settlement, so as to include the whole of the Sierra Leone peninsula. Villages were started in various parts, roads opened up, and education encouraged, while the capital introduced by the men-of-war visiting the station for supplies in the prosecution of their work, created an amount of prosperity hitherto quite unknown in the colony, and unfortunately unassisted by any noticeable local development of trade.

Notwithstanding the Governor's earnest endeavours, all attempts to wed the liberated Africans to agriculture, so as to develop the resources of the colony, failed; since natives are at all times averse from field labour, and the inducements for petty trading were too great to be resisted. As the indentures lapsed, the hoe was abandoned for the basket; the farm labourer became the pedlar: field tillage gave way to hawking; and the negroes revelled in these lazy callings, which gave them cherished opportunities of gossip and idleness, as they vended their paltry wares.

In 1825 Sir Charles MacCarthy lost his life in an engagement with the Ashantis, against overwhelming odds, many of his officers falling bravely fighting by his side; and, his honoured skull and coat are still sworn upon by the Ashantis before engaging in any wars. The colony thus lost the services of a gallant officer, who, by his vigorous upright conduct had done so much for the settlement, and whose courtesy and kindliness of heart won the respect and esteem of officials and natives alike. To this day his memory is revered by the natives, who will ever speak kindly of one whom their parents so much respected. Sir Charles had the good fortune to withstand the rigors of the climate for many years, and his sad death was universally lamented.

Sir Charles Turner, who succeeded him, followed with zeal in the footsteps of his able predecessor. Realising the advantages of extending British influence and opening up the country, he explored the then unknown Sherbro' District, penetrating far up the Boom and Kiltam River, where he made treaties with the native kings, who placed their territory under British rule. To mark the boundary-line of our jurisdiction, Sir Charles Turner shot away a cotton tree by a cannon shot, and the stump is still pointed to with pride by the natives, the record of this act having created such a marked impression upon the native mind that it has become part of the oral history of the District.

At this time the settlement was visited by one of those recurring waves of yellow fever which return to the coast at irregular intervals with deadly effect. Sir Charles Turner succumbed to the climate, after a vigorous reign of only two years, and governor after governor, and a numerous staff of officials, died in rapid succession; while even the natives did not escape from this deadly plague. During the years 1826-1835, five governors and several acting officers died or were invalided; and the colony, already stamped as exceedingly unhealthy, obtained the well-earned but unenviable reputation of being the " White Man's Grave."

The means of communication with the settlement were then so irregular that there were few opportunities of escaping from this fever den when once the disease had enfolded the unfortunate victims in its fatal embrace; and even when a ship did depart, baffling winds and poor diet gave the invalid but indifferent chances of battling with it, while medical science had not then discovered that invaluable febrifuge, Quinine.

The number of slaves annually liberated at Sierra Leone was from three to five thousand, and the expenses attendant upon supplying their wants cost the British Government annually between ten and twenty thousand pounds. This sum was quite independent of other expenses in connection with the government of the colony, and also of the heavy awards in the shape of prize moneys paid to officers and men engaged in suppressing the slave trade. These heavy expenses—which apparently showed every liability to increase, since no apparent diminution appeared in the traffic of slaves—and the proved unhealthiness of the climate, once more raised the question of the abandonment of the colony, which, it had become a recognised fact, could do little or nothing towards its self-support.

We have seen that in 1772 slavery was declared to be unlawful in Great Britian, and that in 1807 the act against the deportation of slaves was passed. The men who had been instrumental in passing these measures had still before them the grand question of Emancipation; and while the Government was vigorously carrying out the act already passed, these philanthropists were pushing forward the grand scheme of abolition.

The winding-up of the Sierra Leone Company, ard the handing over of the colony to the Crown, in a measure revived the beneficent views of the reformers, and gave impetus to a kindred society called the African Institution, having for its object the abolition of slavery throughout the British dominions. Through its indefatigable exertions, every opportunity of exposing the iniquities of slavery was used. Lectures were delivered throughout England by able speakers with their hearts in their work; pamphlets were scattered broadcast; the public utterances of such men as Granville Sharp, Clarkson, Wilberforce, and others, supported by a mass of evidence impossible to refute, were educating the nation on the question. The exertions of these men were stimulated, and their cause received unintended assistance, through the violent actions of the planters and slave-owners in the West Indies, who, in their vindictive antagonism against the missionaries, and by their violent language against the movement, brought the question to a speedier crisis.

A Bill for the amelioration of the condition of slaves in the British Colonies passed the House of Commons in 1823; but as its application was left in the hands of the colonies themselves, it became a dead letter, and only embittered the feelings of the masters towards the slaves. But delay was useless; the knell of slavery had sounded; it had become a doomed system. The petitions in favour of Abolition increased in number and importance, until it became the leading political question of the day.

Mr. Buxton had replaced the venerable Mr. Wilberforce as the leader of the Abolitionists in the House, and availed himself of every opportunity of pushing forward his measure, with that ability and thoroughness which could have but the one triumphant result. After much preparatory skirmishing over the intermediate period, the first Reformed Parliament, opened in 1833, and one of its earliest measures was to pass the Bill for the Abolition of Slavery by a large majority. This Bill received the Royal assent on the 28th August, 1834, and became law on the 1st August following. From that date a system of apprenticeships was introduced— four years for domestic slaves, and six years for farm slaves, when all slavery was to finally cease throughout the British dominions. A sum of twenty millions was voted, to recompense the planters for the losses they suffered by the introduction of this measure.

As England had only monopolised about one-third of the total number of slaves existing, there was for many years but little perceptible difference in the inhuman traffic; and as it was still necessary for its suppression to possess ports on the Coast, it was decided that, notwithstanding its unhealthiness and expense, Sierra Leone should not be abandoned.

England, by her influence with foreign powers, gradually prevailed upon them to abolish slavery, and nation after nation joined in the principles of human Freedom, until the recent American Civil War finally ended in the emancipation of Slavery in that country; thus closing the largest market which had existed in recent years.

With the gradual extinction of slavery beyond the seas the importance of Sierra Leone as a calling station declined, and as the number of war vessels in West African waters were reduced, and the cargoes of slaves captured became fewer and fewer, the colony was at last thrown upon its own resources, and driven to seek for local opportunities of trade.

In less than a century, the population had increased, almost entirely through slave liberation, from a few hundreds to forty thousand souls, and recent acquisitions of territory have now brought it up to more than seventy thousand. No searching census has ever been made. That of 1871 was very loosely carried through, while that of 1881 failed completely in the populous Sherbro' district, through the superstition of the natives and inertness of the local commandant.

This officer, in reporting upon his failure, excused himself on the plea that, though he had failed to carry out the census on that occasion, "he had laid the foundation for future censuses"—a statement so amusing and ridiculous in a West African station, that it deserves to be recorded.

Thus, under the Crown the colony continued its career, and though the expenses incurred in carrying out the policy of Freedom were enormous, the Government, despite the cost, completed the work of emancipation, which in the first instance owed its birthright to the noble exertions of Granville Sharp.

CHAPTER VIII.

EARLY IMPRESSIONS.

SIR SAMUEL ROWE, K.C.M.G., was Governor-in-Chief at the time of my appointment, but he had left the colony upon well-earned leave of absence, a few days before I landed. His office was filled by the Chief Justice, who received me with true English hospitality, courteously making me his table guest, while a brother officer invited me to share his quarters, until I succeeded in finding a house to my liking.

Soon after my arrival, the anniversary of the Queen's birthday came round, and in accordance with the usual custom, all the public offices were closed. But in no other sense was the day a holiday, as the official programme was a long one. At seven a.m. we had to attend a drill parade, while the detachment of the picturesquely-dressed West India Regiment stationed here went through a few simple manœuvres, and then marched past the acting Governor. This parade used up shirt number one.

At eleven there was an official breakfast. This lasted some hours, and effectually finished off shirt number two. At three a levée was held, at which we were formally presented to Her Majesty's representative, who then descended from his high estate with commendable alacrity, and joined us in a loving cup. Shirt number three, worse than predecessors. Our loyalty was increasing.

Finally, at eight p.m. there was an official dinner at Government House, at which a rather amusing *contretemps* occurred. Our local bishop, in pronouncing grace after dinner, stood up. This was a signal for us all to do likewise. He had only proceeded as far as " Oh Lord, for these——," when the band stationed outside struck up " God save the Queen," imagining that the guests had risen to do honour to the loyal toast. The confusion that resulted was indescribable : the bishop worked steadily ahead with his blessing—several of the guests divided their attention between the Church and the bowl—

G

some stuck to the parson—others raised their glasses and said, "The Queen"—while the band continued its loyal strains. This dinner closed the day's proceedings: finished up shirt number four, and many of the guests as well.

On returning with my host to his quarters, we were quite prepared for a good night's rest after the above long day, but such was not to be our good fortune. The servant-boy had also been keeping Her Majesty's birthday, and had not returned with the door-key, though it was midnight, and we were consequently locked out.

There was nothing for it but to sit on the doorstep and wait patiently, without even the solace of a cigar to kill the time. For half an hour this was just endurable. After an hour, when early chanticleers chanted forth their clarion notes, our tempers were worse than our plight. In another hour, spent vainly in trying to sleep on a very rough doorstep, oblivious of dress-clothes, we became frantic. So I inquired "whether it was not possible to force the door?" and at it we went in desperation, shoulder to shoulder. But it was obdurate and massive:

however, the adjoining panelling seemed weaker, and in this, with the help of a large stone, we forced a hole, through which we ignominiously crawled, and soon forgot our enforced vigil in sound sleep, just as the early dawn was spreading its dull-grey light over the distant hills.

About seven I heard the most piteous howling proceeding from the next room, and a glance at my mangled clothes recalled the sad realities of a few hours ago. I jumped up and looked through the verandah window at the proceedings. The delinquent boy was being held at arm's-length by my irate companion. The other hand, with a cane in it, was upraised, while the fixed eye spoke volumes. But the youngster yelled so loudly and waltzed round so energetically, that the descent could not be made on the spot particularly desired. When the arm did fall, however, it had a magic effect, for with one wrench the boy was across the room and out of the door, when the following dialogue took place:

Host (bawling angrily): "Tom!"

Tom (at a very respectful distance and hovering near the door): "Sah!"

Host: "Come here at once, sir."

Tom: "Oh, Lor', massa, no moa—sah,—I beg you; true, true."

Host: "Come on, sir. I've not touched you yet, you young scoundrel."

Tom: "Oh, massa, I berry, berry sorry" (going on knees near the door); "I nebber do it again. I take lilly drop for de Queen's buff-day, an' no sabbe de time.—Hoo ——"

Host: "Well, I'll fine you half a month's wages" (tremendous howling at this); now go next door to other massa, and beg his pardon. I hope he'll flog you if he can catch you."

I accordingly slipped back into my room, when Tom entered, looking very submissive.

Tom: "Massa, I do beg you dis time, I do."

Myself: "Yes, that's all very well, but your master said I was to flog you, and I think you thoroughly deserve it."

Tom (howling again): "Oh, Lor', hoo—hoo hoo—o;—other massa been flog me too much a'ready. Hoo—hoo—hoo!"

Myself: "Why, you young rascal, he hardly touched you."

Tom: "Oh, massa, for true, he been catch my arm an' make me dance round de room."

Myself (adopting the vernacular): "Yes, Tom, and now you catch de stick, which make you dance round de room;" and I called the cook.

Cook, entering with suspicious readiness, and quite prepared to assist in the chastisement of one of his own species: "Sah!"

Myself: "Catch Tom, and hold him tight while I flog him."

Cook: "A'right, massa, nebber fear dis cook can hold him true."

Tom (yelling vociferously): "Oh, Lor'! hoo—hoo—hoo! I beg you dis time, massa—I beg you ——"

Myself: "Now, Tom, you're going to get six cuts with that cane." (Tom casts a lingering glance in the direction of the cane.) "But if you prefer it, I will flog you with a towel," —as an afterthought enters my head.

Tom: "Wid towel, massa! I nebber been flog dat way before."

Myself: "Yes, with a towel. Come, which will you have? be quick!"

Tom (with considerable interest). "Which hurt de mos', massa?"

Myself: "You young rogue. How should I know?"

Tom (in wheedling tones to the cook). "Which you tink de bes', cookie, eh! for not hurt too much?"

Cook: "Golly, me no sabbe; try tree (three) ob each, dat's de bes' way." And Tom, quite forgetful of his howling, decided to try the towel first.

Myself: "Now, cook, put his head between your legs and hold him tight."

Cook: "In chokee—eh, massa—a'right, nebber fear, dis chile hold 'um tight for true; he learn dis in de galley."

Myself: "In the galley—what's that?"

Cook: "De kitchen on bode de man-ob-war is called de galley, 'spects ebery white man sabbe dat."

By this time Tom was in position, with head well secured between the cook's knees, and his arms round the cook's legs; so, carefully judging the distance, I made the first flick with a damp towel, and just missed the spot aimed at.

Tom: "That na number one whack, massa."

The next shot was a better one, and the expressive click of the towel as its well-measured end caught the tightened breeches of the boy's broad beam had scarcely sounded before Tom, with a yell, threw up his head and shoulders with such vigour that the cook went sprawling on the floor, while the boy, with hands clapped to his nether quarters, bolted out of the room.

A short while afterwards, having to pass near the kitchen, I heard much laughter going on. I looked in, and there was Master Tom pantomiming the late scene with a small boy between his legs "in chokee," while the cook, with a dish-cloth, was preparing to administer the punishment. Catching sight of me, Tom's face assumed a look of agony which would have made his fortune in melodrama, and with his hands he expressively caressed the seat of his recent injury, the other youngster seizing the golden opportunity to beat a rapid retreat by a side-door.

I soon found a house which had the advantage of being partly furnished. The owner promised that it should be thoroughly cleaned up by the end of the week, if I would only advance half a month's rent. This I readily agreed to, and looked forward with pleasure to the prospect of getting settled. When the day arrived, I sent the boy and cook whom I had engaged, to the house with my things, and after office hours I followed. To my chagrin I found the boy in the street, perched on the top of my boxes and bales, indulging in a flow of small-talk with a gaping crowd, while pigs, dogs, and roosters added a farm-yard appearance to the scene.

Myself (angrily): "Alfonso! (the boy's name) where's the cook?"

Alfonso: "Me don't sabbe; he no lib (live) since de morning."

Myself (horrified at this example of West African climate on one of its own children): "Why didn't you come and tell me?"

Alfonso: "An' leave de clothes (for so he described my boxes and portmanteaux). You nebber see 'um more if I did that. No, massa, we wait here all day until you come."

Myself: "Well, put the things inside the house, and then you can go and see about the cook. Why didn't you carry them into the house before?"

Alfonso: "'Cause de door lock."

Myself: "Yes, but where's Mr. Thompson, the landlord?"

Alfonso: "Me don't see him, but 'specks he lib dere." (Casting his eyes towards the house).

Myself: "Yes, I know that he lived there, you idiot. But where is he now?"

Alfonso (looking very hard at me): "Massa, I done tell you a'ready that he lib."

Myself (irritably, giving up the argument, and pointing down the street) : "Of course he lives, you stupid. Go and find the man at once, and bring him to me."

Alfonso: "A'right, massa; you mind de clothes." (And ascending the house-steps, he began battering the door).

Myself: "What is the use of doing that, boy, if he is not in?"

Alfonso: "I no hab tell you, sah, dat he lib."

And without further ado he continued playing a devil's tattoo on the structure. At length his efforts were successful, and Mr. Thompson opened the door. I saw that he was hopelessly intoxicated, while a glimpse into the house showed it to be in disorder and uncleaned, and several square-faced bottles lying on the floor.

Landlord: "Hic—what do you mean, sah, by —hic—making dis—hic—noise on my door?"

Myself: "Why, I have come to take possession of the house that you promised to have cleaned up, instead of which I find it in a filthy state, and you drunk."

Landlord: "What you mean—hic—to abuse me, sah—eh? Get off my—hic—premises—else I go law you."

Myself (triumphantly): "Now, here's your receipt for half a month's rent, so you clear out, and the boy will try and clean up the place. You can send to-morow and finish it."

Landlord: "To-day Saturday, an' I—hic—take my rest. To-morrow de sabbath, an' I go wusship de Lor', my—hic—God, an' work for no man. So you can go 'way, white man, an'—hic—no 'buse more."

Seeing that it was hopeless, that the house was in an uninhabitable condition, and feeling forcibly the truth of the adage that "possession is nine-tenths of the law," I formed part of an undignified procession back to my host's quarters, and explained my dilemma. I added seriously, "But this is not the worst, for the poor fellow I engaged as cook has died since the morning; so my boy tells me."

Alfonso: "No, massa, I no tell you nuffin' like dat: cook no dead. Golly! I nebber sed dat."

EARLY IMPRESSIONS.

Myself (rather aghast): "Why, you rascal, when I asked you where the cook was, you said he hadn't lived since the morning." And turning to my host, I continued: "and he seemed quite unconcerned about it."

My host now began to laugh heartily, and I assumed that inexplicable expression which implies, "What the deuce are you laughing at?"

Host, to Alfonse: "So de cook no lib since de morning, eh, boy?"

Alfonso: "No, sah."

Myself: "There, I told you so; so he *is* dead then?"

Alfonso: "No, sah, he no dead."

Host: "No, he's alive and kicking."

Myself (feeling very much like "Cox" in the well-known dialogue): "Well, well, if you can tell me how a man can't live, or 'lib' to use the local pronunciation, and yet be alive, I—I shall be rather astonished."

My host then explained that in "pidgin English" "live" was synonymous with being at home. For instance, if I went to any house and asked if the tenant was at home, I should be told "Yes," whether he was in at the time or not. But if I asked instead, "Does he lib," the "yes" would imply that he was within. So, therefore, the cook's "not libbing since the morning," merely meant that he had not been near the house since the morning, and was still absent, instead of the mournful construction I had given to the words.

Innumerable mistakes have occurred through this local peculiarity in phraseology, and I have seen a naval officer, newly arrived on the station, roundly abusing a native policeman for having answered in the affirmative when asked if the Governor was at home; which was found not to be the case when he arrived at the house. It is not unlikely that this phrase has arisen from the frequent inquiries made by officers and passengers passing through, "whether so-and-so is still alive"? and the natives have thus adopted it as a question of local presence, instead of the usual meaning of the phrase. Another singular expression, peculiar to the place, is, "What, you come to take fire, then?"—meaning that your visit is a very short one. This originates from the custom among the poorer classes, who are frequently short of matches, or in out-of-the-way places, where igniting a fire is a matter of such difficulty that the natives arrange among themselves to keep one perpetually slumbering. Consequently anyone wanting a light pays a hurried visit and carries away a piece of lighted wood. Hence, if you pay a very short visit to a native place, the expression means that they think you are hurrying away too soon, and is also in a measure a courteous hint that your presence is agreeable. After a few months I soon acquired a smattering of "Sierra Leone English," as it is called, and which is incomprehensible, for some time, to a new arrival.

The cook I had engaged now put in an appearance, and said that he had been only able to procure a "berry tender chicken" for dinner. Without farther ado he produced a wretched cockerel, which had all the appearance of having been plucked alive. The fowl was, I thought, meant by nature to be a white one; but, beyond a few scraggy feathers on the neck, and a thin line of quills on the wings, he was quite featherless, while the deep scarlet of the flesh convinced me that he had been illtreated. So I sternly inquired whether he had been guilty of such gross cruelty. The cook looked very astonished, and said "he had done nuffin to de bird."

"I am very glad to hear it, cook; but where did you buy that wretched thing."

"He no poor, massa; he good chicken dis kind; me no hab de trouble to pluck him, an' he no can fly away."

"Yes; but who plucked all the feathers out?" I said. "Go and kill it at once."

"De bird berry well, massa; not want to kill 'um now that massa go dine Government House."

I ordered its immediate execution, and said, "he was on no account to buy another in such a condition," while I resolved to report such cruel proceedings, with a view of having them stopped.

At dinner in the evening I waxed eloquent over the wanton cruelty thus inflicted, as I thought, to save time and to prevent the wretched thing flying away. There was a general laugh at my expense, as it was explained that these featherless birds were only a peculiar species by no means uncommon in tropical countries; but there is no reason to suppose that they are any more tender than the ordinary fowl, unless the extra exposure can make them so. My mistake in this matter led to a description of my house-hunting experiences, which my host related in a very graphic and amusing manner, for the benefit of the rest of the guests.

CHAPTER IX.

AN UNPLEASANT ENCOUNTER.

The landlord having exhausted his potations, soon gave up possession, and sent a message expressing regret that pressure of business had prevented him cleaning up the house by the time agreed upon.

I therefore moved in and started housekeeping on my own account. At the end of the month there were several applicants for the rent. One old girl said that the house belonged to her sister-in-law, and that I was to pay her the balance, and not Mr. Thompson. She made out such a good case that I would certainly have paid up had not another female claimant arrived After a somewhat wordy war between the two, she informed me that her aunt had given her special charge of the house, and that I must only pay her.

Presently my boy announced that "anudder coloured lady" wished to see me; and as I now began to enter into the fun of the thing, I told him to "show her up." After shaking hands with me with easy familiarity, and hoping I was quite well, she said, " How d'ye do, sistah?" to my other two guests. Her claim was, that being "de business partner ob de landlady" who was away trading up the rivers, that she was managing all her affairs, and that I should pay her and her only.

Then a lively dispute arose among them, which was to me "high Dutch," so rapidly did they carry it on and wrangle in "pidgin English." At last I managed to put a stop to it by declaring my intention of not paying any of them; a decision they apparently had not expected. In reply to an interrogatory, they were unanimous in agreeing that I was not to pay Mr. Thompson, who had only been permitted to use the house rent free during the owner's absence, and who would certainly spend the rent on himself in drink. In this perplexing state of affairs, I determined to constitute myself into a temporary Court of Chancery pending the return of or written instructions from the actual owner.

In the evening Mr. Thompson personally applied for the balance of rent for the month, and I acquainted him with my decision. From his appearance, and the unpleasant odour of strong drink, it was evident that he had been again in luck's way, or had already discounted the money he had hoped to obtain from me. Finding that I was obdurate, he became noisy, threatening, and abusive, in turns, until I sent for a policeman, before whose arrival he took his departure with the parting scathing remark that I " was a nice sort of white man, to take a house from a coloured gentleman and not pay the rent for it."

An opportunity occurred shortly afterwards by which I was able to go shares in a house with a brother officer, so I moved again, and found it much more agreeable than living alone. Here everything went smoothly by day, but during the night our troubles were unendurable, through the continuous barking and howling of a pack of pariah dogs, belonging to several natives, who occupied a few small huts in the vicinity. Our repeated messages and threats were alike ignored, and the nuisance became so persistent that both myself and my companion were affected in health and spirits through want of sleep, and I was strongly advised to shoot these pests.

All other attempts to check the nuisance having failed, early one morning I sallied forth into the deserted street with my gun, determined to bring matters to an issue. As I approached the hovels, the barking was renewed with redoubled energy. But owing to a deep shadow cast by the wattle fencing surrounding the small compound, I was unable to see the dogs, and I hesitated firing in the direction of the sound, for fear of doing other damage. So, gathering a few pebbles, and taking a line with an adjacent dead wall, I threw them inside, in order to bring the brutes into the open, where it would be perfectly safe to fire.

The shower of gravel brought out a man, instead of the dogs, who rushed up to me, and in most abusive language demanded " what I was doing so near his fence at that hour?" With his words, I felt a heavy lunge pass close to my arm; and as he withdrew his arm, mine was again knocked with the weapon, or stick, he had so vigorously thrust at me. I retired a few steps as soon as I recovered from the surprise of this sudden and unexpected onslaught, and explained to the man that he must keep his dogs quiet; when he again poured out a volley of abuse, asserting that I had come to rob his house, but that he would soon settle me; adding, in an insulting voice, and in language quite unfit for print, that if I did not at once go away, he would shove his spear through me.

By this time a heavy cloud that had obscured the moon passed away. The man was perfectly naked, and was armed with a bamboo pole about eight feet long, surmounted by an old-fashioned bayonet; and it was with this weapon that he had made such a determined attack. But for that dark cloud which had made everything indistinct, I should have most certainly been run completely through the body, so fiercely had the thrust been made. Even as it was, I was by no means free from danger, and the seriousness of the situation forced itself upon me.

Here was I, with a loaded gun in the still hours of an early morning, under the light of a few twinkling stars, confronted by a man armed with a formidable spear, who had already made one savage attack, and was threatening, in violent language, to repeat it. Intuitively I glanced at my gun, and while grasping it still more firmly, I felt afraid to think of using it, even in the strictest self-defence, while if I walked away, the man would probably again attack me. Several women now appeared at the doors of the hovels; and, feeling that the most judicious thing to do was to talk, I called to them to come out and take their friend away. The women did as I told them, and after a little persuasion the man retired with them, muttering threats of what he would have done had they not interfered, and what he would do next time I came to "rob his house."

As I left the scene of this awkward encounter, I broke out into a cold sweat, as I thought of the serious complications which must have followed had I, acting in the strictest self-defence, been compelled to shoot this wretched fellow; while I could not but feel devoutly thankful for that fleeting cloud that had darkened the earth, and thereby certainly saved my life.

Next day the matter was reported to the police, and my assailant was had up before the court. It was proved that he was a noted bad character, and in a constant state of delirium, through drink, when he was quite unaccountable for his actions: all of which showed that my escape was still more fortunate. The spear was confiscated; the man was fined a small sum, and his relations had to give security for his future good behaviour. The mud hovels, on inspection, were found to be in a horribly unsanitary condition, and rather than put the place in order, these unpleasant neighbours and their pack of howling curs left the town.

My early experiences of some of the Africans were thus anything but satisfactory; and having, in common with most Englishmen who know nothing of the matter, imagined that the natives were probably victimized and oppressed, I was thus rudely awakened to a condition of affairs I never supposed could have existed; and I began to feel that it is not quite safe to introduce the bush savage to all the freedom of immediate civilization.

By now I had become well set in the groove of official life; but it soon became apparent that an officer's titular appointment was by no means an indication of the work he would have to do; for, owing to the number of officials absent on their well-earned leave, and others laid low with fever, it was necessary, in order to carry on the work of the colony, to make the duties interchangeable, and thus keep it under by the assiduity of those officials who were still at their posts. At times the colony is almost bereft of officers, and it is by no means an exceptional thing for one of them to have to take charge of two or even three separate departments, notwithstanding that the officer's own titular office may be very short-handed.

The office hours in the Secretariat and Treasury were from 7 a.m to 9 a.m., and from 11 a.m to 5 p.m., without any relaxation on Saturday. These hours were far too excessive in such an enervating climate, especially when it is borne in mind that even before and after those hours, an officer is frequently compelled to attend to any work that may arise requiring immediate attention. The native clerks very much resented these long hours. For years previously they had been working from the traditional ten to four of official life, and it soon became apparent to me that, notwithstanding these long hours, they were doing far less work than might easily have been accomplished in the ordinary time. Expostulation and argument were in vain; they always appeared to be at work, but it was the parliamentary train of labour, and not the willing express speed of men desirous of doing their duty. Sir Samuel Rowe had made the alteration, and his locum tenens would not interfere. The result was that the brunt of this dissatisfaction fell most heavily on the English officials, who had a quantity of other work thrust upon them, and it became a matter of difficulty to carry on the ordinary office routine.

It was an agreeable change to me, therefore, when a brother officer returned from leave, as it enabled me, after many months close confinement to office work, to slacken my exertions for a short while. I consequently managed to get away of an afternoon, and obtain some of the poor sport the neighbourhood afforded. A few bush fowl (a kind of partridge) was all that one could get; but these were extremely wild, while the dense bush with huge boulders of stone at every step made locomotion difficult, and good bags an impossibility, in a climate where the slightest exertion produces profuse perspiration.

The neighbourhood for several miles round the town was soon very familiar to me, and in climbing the mountains in search of deer, the picturesque beauty of the magnificent estuary, branching out into many different forks, irresistibly developed a desire to go further afield in search of game and adventure.

An opportunity soon occurred of buying a small boat, and I had her rigged up according to my own design. Her keel was only eighteen feet long, and on this I had an additional false keel bolted, as she was too small for a centreboard. She could pull four oars, and there was yet room for two passengers to sit comfortably in the stern. A large sprit sail, made of the lightest material, so as to hold the gentlest breeze, and an awning with an inner lining of green, and with side curtains, were next made, and the little craft was complete. She sailed splendidly, and I looked with pride on her trim appearance, all arranged at a trifling expense by a little ingenuity. Her total cost was under twenty pounds, and I sold her at a profit, after repeated attacks of fever had reluctantly compelled me to give up my boating expeditions.

Now that I was able to indulge my roving desires, the river, with its network of creeks and islands, soon became quite familiar to me, and I found villages scattered in odd places, up dank and narrow creeks, some of which had not been visited for years. My entry, with my Newfoundland dog, to one of these one early morning, created quite a stampede, and in a few minutes the narrow street was deserted and all doors closed; the women and children having run away at the unusual sight of a white man accompanied with such a huge companion. In vain my boy looked about for some one to ask whether there was any sport to be had close by. At last I directed him to force his way into a small compound, from which I heard subdued voices, while I sat on a boulder of stone, awaiting the result of his inquiries.

The boy's report was unsatisfactory: there were no cassada plantations in the vicinity, and my time was too short to wander aimlessly about. It appeared that most of the men had gone away to work, and the women were afraid, not only of the big dog, but of myself. Yet this village is within ten miles of Freetown, and lies, unknown and unnamed, under a silk cotton-tree up a narrow creek, accessible to boats at high tide only.

I therefore returned to the "Wave," determined to give up all thoughts of a partridge breakfast, and to push on for Waterloo, some twenty miles higher up the creek, whither I was bound on a visit to our local manager, a charming old gentleman, who, like many others, decided to put in that one more year before retiring on a well deserved pension : a year, the end of which found his name among those who had passed over to the majority in the settlement in which he had worked so well.

On returning to the wharf, as all landing-places are called in West Africa, though they are nothing but a strip of filthy mud, I was carried to the boat through the thick slime, and we started back for the main river. One of the men called my attention to a monkey in the mangrove bush some distance ahead ; so, directing the boat to be pulled as noiselessly as possible, I stood up and let fly, at about sixty yards distance. There was a shrill scream, and much discordant cawing, as a number of birds, disturbed by the noise of the explosion, rose above the bushes ; and with the spare barrel I bowled over a stork, which was well within range. One of the men waded ashore, to search for the monkey, and he soon returned with a dead mangrove monkey, to which a small baby monkey was clinging with human-like action, while it chattered away and screamed in its thin piping tones. The poor little thing was also wounded, and it was pitable to see how it clung to its dead mother, trying to hide behind it whenever I attempted to separate them. I tried to give it some condensed milk, but it was useless, and it died alongside of its mother, just as we reached the mouth of the creek.

I had left Freetown at three in the morning. It was now about six, and the morning sea breeze was already coming up in fitful puffs. Far over the land, as though ascending from the heart of the "dark continent," was a glorious golden ball, perceptibly spreading its brilliant garish light over the fleecy sky. The huge silk cotton-trees, at this season laden with tufts of downy silk, were standing out boldly as landmarks of nature on the numerous promonteries jutting out from different parts of the wide lagoon, striking fantastic shadows on the water as the sun gold-tipped the higher branches. Below, as far as the eye could see, the ever-green mangrove made a never-ending fringe along the banks of the mainland and islets, except where a thin streak of sunlit water showed that still another creek branched off into the low-lying land. It was truly a pretty picture, made much more charming by the brilliant plumage of the kingfishers, flitting to and fro in search of their morning meal; while, on a low stretch of mud industrious aquatic birds were making their morning meal, guarded by the ever vigilant curlew, whose occasional plaintive whistle warned his companions that there was danger afloat on the bosom of the placid river.

CHAPTER X.

A FIGHT WITH AN ALLIGATOR.

"Up sail and awning" was the order, and in a few minutes the "Wave" was skimming merrily over the surface of the wide lagoon, with eased sheet, as the breeze was almost dead astern.

In the fore-part of the boat a Rippingill's stove was burning brightly, giving out a savoury smell of an early breakfast, for which I was quite ready. But I could see that the men were ill at ease, as they talked in low tones among themselves; so I inquired what was the matter.

"Massa, I no tink you can fetch Waterloo until dis evening, as de tide's running down."

"I know that, Davis, as the creek will be dry when we get up: I arranged that way on purpose, hoping to have some alligator shooting at low tide."

"I tink, massa, it be better to go back to n'a

town (n'a, the), and come up some day wid de tide straight."

"I shall do nothing of the kind. I particularly came up with this tide so as to have plenty of time on the way. But come," I added, as I noticed their dissatisfied looks, "what does this mean?" For it is African nature never to say exactly what they are driving at straight out.

"Massa, bery bad gre-gre been happen dis morning."

"Why, what was that?" I said, interested at once.

"Massa, you been kill n'a picken (baby) monkey."

"Well, it was quite accidental," I replied, rather untruthfully; "besides, the gre-gre would overtake us in Freetown just as much as it would here. Never run away from danger, my man," I added loftily.

"Massa, p'raps dis only black man gre-gre, and not white man gre-gre?"

"Very well; you men, then—as the white man killed the monkey and not the black man—you need have no fear." I felt I was becoming quite an adept at native argument. "But come, get Tom to cook your rice, now that my breakfast is passed down."

"Bery good, massa, we go wid you; but something bad sure to happen before we get home again."

Alas! the pleasant coolness of the early morning lasts but an hour, when king Sol comes out with a force that drives even the tropical birds to take shelter in the thick bush; and as I reclined lazily beneath the double awning, I looked with wonder at the boatmen with heads uncovered, basking in the very heat which to me would bring almost certain death. Africans positively like the sun, and they can work under it throughout the day, or lie asleep in it, without raising a single blister, or feeling any inconvenience from its powerful rays. The bright green mangrove flies were extremely troublesome; and as their bite draws blood, these pests had to be carefully watched as they returned again and again to the attack, with all the wariness of the mosquito.

The long stretches of mud began to show themselves as the tide rapidly ebbed, and the disagreeable stench arising from this fetid slush, as the sun began to tell upon it, made it advisable to take mid-stream, so as to escape as much as possible from the offensive smell. It is this rank putrified mud which makes the Settlement so unhealthy; and the shallowness of this otherwise magnificent estuary, combined with the unhealthiness thus caused, very much detracts from the pleasures of boating in the upper reaches of its wide creeks and rivers.

The water is thick with mud and spawn—so thick that on no occasion, either of low or high tide—can one see below its surface. The boat was now in a part of the river infested with thousands of alligators; but in vain we scanned the muddy banks for that log-like looking reptile which is such a terror to the natives.

At length we rapidly approached the top of the lagoon, where it branches off into many different creeks—that to Waterloo being on the right bank, up which we afterwards proceeded, when the tide returned and restored it to a navigable water way. In front lay "Fish Island"—a small sand-bank on which a wretched shanty is erected. Here, during the season, natives dry the "bungay," a "skunk fish" so much relished by them, but the rotten smell of which is most nauseating to European stomachs.

I

But the island was deserted, for the curing season was over, and had happily left none of its flavour behind. Away on the other side of the creek lies the Quiah country, governed by the Queens of Quiah, who resolutely defended their territory when it became necessary that we should annex a portion of it. They—for it is a triplicate Gynarchy—still rule over a very large portion of territory and enjoy a subsidy from the government for "British Quiah," while they succeed in maintaining law and order in native Quiah, far better than many potentates of the sterner sex. The boat was run full tilt into the mud of "Fish Island," and after beating the water all round, to drive away any alligator that might by chance be hovering about, I was carried on shore, and sought relief from the sun under a clump of palms throwing out a welcome shade. I noticed that in landing the things the men were very quick, and that they had evidently made up their minds to avoid all risk of danger from alligators or gre-gres.

My boys soon had a fire burning; and creeping round the island, I bowled over a brace of curlew, whose whistle in this instance brought about their own doom. About a mile to the

A FIGHT WITH AN ALLIGATOR. 117

right lay "Rowesville," just before the entrance to the shallow creek leading to Waterloo. This is an estate named after Governor Rowe, who gave the land to a native, in order that he might introduce an improved system of agriculture: but he appeared to be content with the profits obtained from it in the good old style. Some hundred yards in front, towards Quiah, there was a solitary canoe, from which a man and boy were fishing for the small flat-fish with which the river abounds. It was almost low tide, and round no part of the island was there sufficient water for nearly fifty yards to float the " Wave," so she lay helplessly on one side, with the receding river lapping musically against her.

A stone made a convenient table. On this a napkin was spread, and I was soon engaged in another feed, while I looked round with pleasure on the picturesque landscape, as the broad expanse of the creek wandered into many small bays. The men were lazily lolling about, waiting for their turn to tuck in, and talking about the friends they would meet at Waterloo, and the evening of pleasure they had evidently made up their mind to have among them.

"Well, Davis, n'a gre-gre not do any harm yet?" I said, in slightly sarcastic tones.

"No, massa, I hope no trouble can catch us dis time."

But as the words were uttered, a wild cry for help broke out upon the still scene.

One of my men rushed round from the back of the island and cried out: "Massa, n'a dug-out upset, an' de man calling for help." As he spoke, a shrill halloo! and the cry of the boy again heard from that direction.

I followed the men round the island, apprehending nothing, and expecting to see the occupants of the canoe wading ashore, or again inside of it. The man was standing in about four feet of water and mud, with paddle in hand, pushing and striking at the water, while the canoe floated slowly down with the tide. The boy, still screaming, swam rapidly towards the far shore.

"But why let the canoe drift away upside-down, when he can so easily regain it?" I said, speaking more to myself than the men. Yet, as I spoke, there was a commotion in the waters and the man, a powerful fellow, began hitting out with all his might at a huge dripping body,

"I FIRED WIDELY SEVERAL TIMES IN QUICK SUCCESSION."
See p. 119.

now slowly raising itself a few paces before him. " By Heavens! an alligator!" I cried, as the monster stood high out of the water, the ugly head craned forward, and the two front legs battling with the doomed negro.

"My gun and shot-bag quick!" and, suiting the action to the word, I tore round to the rock where I had left them, and returned panting with the exertion, and earnestly excited, that I might be in time.

Yes, there they were still, about eighty yards off, the man fighting for dear life, hitting out hard and strong, at the massive saurian but a few feet from him. The blows fell harmlessly upon the thick head and body of the brute, while the man endeavoured to back farther away. There was not a foot between them now, and it was impossible to fire, as with anxious heart I dropped on one knee, and tried in vain to take a true sight. It was impossible to do so, as the man's body was constantly covering that of the alligator in their struggle, so I fired widely several times in quick succession, in the vain hope of frightening the beast away.

But my shots were unheeded, for they were soon absolutely entangled in an unequal wrestling match, as with a quick movement, the huge alligator threw itself upon the wretched man. "The boat!" I said, but my men shook their heads. She was lying useless on an oozy bed of mud, and no amount of poling would move her into deep water within at least an hour. So I continued firing, and then rushed desperately into the water, with an idea of wading towards the man. But it was useless. Ere I proceeded ten yards, the mud and slush were up to my middle, and I could barely move my feet; so I returned to the shore. It was too late to do anything, for slowly, but surely, the alligator was gaining ground; its neck and body were craning over the man's shoulder, while he tried to dig it off with his useless weapon.

There was a momentary struggle, a sort of spreading wriggle, as though the alligator was putting still more weight into its body; a faint cry, a splash, and the water threw around a few circular rings as they sank beneath its surface. In vain I watched the water, with faint hope of seeing the man rise once more to renew the unequal contest. Not a sign nor vestige again appeared, and below the dark surface of the silent stream the brute lay sprawling above its unhappy victim until he was drowned.

In sorrow, and sickened, I walked away, leaving my almost untasted food in disgust, as I tried to believe that the dreadful encounter that had taken place was nothing but a horrid vision. How bravely and well the man had fought, trying so hard to keep the brute at arm's length, as he rained blow after blow upon its tough body. With what mighty power the alligator had closed upon him, and in less than five minutes in all, had overpowered the defenceless man by the sheer weight of its heavy body, and borne him below the dirty river, there to feast upon its hapless victim. In the far distance the boy's head could be seen as he struggled for the shore, on which he soon landed, and climbing into a protecting tree, he shouted a faint halloo, to show that he was safe. It would have been nearer for him to have landed at Fish Island, but the dreaded alligator and the man were fighting between, and that, probably, made him strike out for the Quiah shore.

CHAPTER XI.

ALLIGATORS STILL.

"MASSA, massa, n'a tide coming up fast, and good for start now," said one of the men; and I jumped up from a disturbed sleep into which I had fallen, in which visions of alligators attacking men were incongruously mixed up with Hyde Park Corner in a dreamily sane manner. I must have been asleep several hours, for the "Wave" was dancing on the rippling water, with her mast and sail neatly stowed, and the long bamboo sprit and boom hanging over the side in the loops made for them, so as not to hamper the little craft. The blue ensign, with the Union Jack in the corner, and the badge of the colony—an elephant and a palm tree emblazoned on a yellow ground in its centre,—showed up fitfully as the flag fluttered in the gentle breeze.

Everything was ready for a start, so, mounting pig-aback, I was soon under the comfortable awning, and the men pulled cheerfully towards the creek. I steered for the place where the poor boy had landed when he gained the opposite shore; but my men informed me that a passing canoe had already picked him up, and had then gone towards Quiah. I next directed the boat to the spot where the dreadful encounter had occurred but a few hours since. It was impossible to see below the surface of the sluggish water, and one of the men searched in vain with the boat-hook for the remains of the unfortunate fellow.

The boat's head was again turned towards the creek. On the right we passed Rowesville, but did not stop, as time was pressing. To the left was a large strip of mud not yet covered by the rising tide. This divides the narrow creek up which lies Waterloo from the broad but shallow expanse leading to the native town of Mobolo. Curlew and plover, together with storks and cranes, and flocks of the little mud-larks, were industriously searching for food ere the rising tide drove them to the mangrove bush. But as I was in hopes of having a shot at an alligator further on, they were left undisturbed as the boat entered the fringed edge of the creek.

This creek is so narrow, and the bushes and trees are so dense, that the awning was no longer required; and after it was stowed away, I gave the tiller to one of the men, since the tide was only yet half up, and to keep in the navigable channel of the serpentine stream required a previous knowledge of its winding course. In some places we almost touched the side-banks with the oars; in others the overhanging trees overlapped, forming a picturesque colonnade of deep green, through which the sun cast fitful rays on the dark-shadowed stream. The busy hum of insect life kept up a perpetual singing, intermixed with the hoarse tones of the bullfrogs, in their incessant croaking, which was hushed as the plash of the oars warned them of approaching danger.

Humming-birds, with their beautiful plumage and bright little eyes, fluttered about with almost cage-like tameness, and paddy-birds and banana suckers of different hues twittered away with pleasing notes, as they hopped from branch to branch. Surely this is a paradise of birds, I thought, as the beautiful blue-green kingfisher, with its bright red beak, sat insolently on a high branch, giving out his shrill note of defiance, while a still fiercer-looking species, with black and white stripes and smaller body, flew more wildly by.

"Massa," cried the man steering, "you see dat hump of sand in mid stream, n'a alligator lying on top." And there, sure enough, not twenty yards ahead, on a sand-heap, was a slimy scaly mass, its tail and head buried under water, its body lying athwart this bed, on which a faint ray of sun glinted with pleasing warmth. I quickly slipped a couple of Macquoid bullets into my gun—my last two, having fired away the others in the morning; and telling the men to back water, I passed up to the bow of the boat, and rested the muzzle on the boat's edge. But she was not very steady, and as there was no sign of restlessness on the part of the scaly brute, I gave the boatmen orders to pull "softly, softly," for a few more strokes.

It would not do to venture further with the oars; so the rowing was stopped, and the boat glided on imperceptibly towards the alligator,

Unfortunately, its right side was towards me, and I could not clearly trace the outline of its front legs, but I aimed well forward and low down, and fired both barrels at the huge beast. There was an instantaneous upheaval of sand, mud, and water, a great splashing, and the alligator slowly tumbled off the mound on the opposite side.

"Now pull away for it," I shouted in great excitement; but it was short lived, as we soon stuck hard-and-fast in the mud, and no amount of poling would drive the boat further on. "Well, we must get out, that's all," I said.

"No debbil fear, massa, nobody can do dat; too much alligator lib for dat, an' de mud too thick."

This was obviously true, so I gave up that idea. "Well, we can wait for the high tide," I determined; but even this did not please the men.

"Bother your gre-gre alligator—pull on,' I cried angrily. "When will you men who profess to be christians understand that your gre-gre is humbug, and that you're a 'nonsense foolish fellow' not to see it." ("A nonsense foolish fellow" being the acme of abuse, and reflecting on the person referred to, more than any amount of hard swearing).

"Massa, wese (we is) christians, for true, and sabbe book palaver (the bible); but massa, n'a gre-gre lib all de same; every one can tell you dat in dis country. Hadn't I told you dis morning, massa, when you kill de pickin monkey, dat someting bad gwin to happen, and didn't it true?—Look at dat poor black man which we see fight n'a alligator an' get kill. Massa (decidedly spoken), dat alligator not alligator at all, but fetish alligator."

"Why, what makes you suppose that?"

"Massa, ain't dis n'a black man country? an' plenty tings lib here which p'raps no lib in Hinglan' (England). You been see dat your shooten' no frighten dat alligator away. No— cause why? Cause dat jus' gre-gre alligator!"

"Well what's the difference between a gre-gre alligator and any other, my man?"

"Massa, plenty witch lib in dis country who sabbe country medicine too much. If dey like, dey can put stuff on de road, an' will it to kill one person and not anudder. Ain't he able to make man's arm so stiff dat he can't move it? and when he want to kill person, can't he make him into alligator or tiger, to kill other person? No, massa, dat n'a gre-gre alligator, we'se sure, an' tho' I'se sorry for dat other black man, I'se glad it not been one of me."

The natives use the word witch for both male and female medicine folk, and one might as well try to turn the Niagara as convince them, even those who have been educated in England, that fetish does not exist. So I listened with wonder to the man's somewhat lengthy argument, all of which tended to show that the unfortunate accident we had witnessed in the morning, and the coincidence of its following upon the death of the baby monkey, had, if possible, gone to strengthen their superstitious belief in gre-gres. The event would certainly lose none of its fetish flavour in being told hereafter to those already so thoroughly imbued with the fixed belief in evil spirits.

The man was inclined to be communicative on the subject of Fetish lore, so, by an indirect question, I easily led him to continue his interesting remarks.

"As you no bery incline' to b'lieve in dese witches, massa, I can tell you story about dis bery place Waterloo, which you no p'raps hab heard, and which happen lilly (little) while before you come."

No, Davis, I've not heard any story. By all means go on."

"Well, massa, der been one man hyar who been married country fashion, with coloured woman for several years, an' dey ketch picken (had children). In dis country person can lib like dat togedder until dey save enough money to hab 'spectable weddin', an' den dey marry English fashion, an' make big dance an' palaver with all der friends. Well, dese two peoples been lib like dis for about tree (three) years, puttin' lilly money by in de ole kettle ebery month, so dat when it swell big enough dey can celebrate de nuptials."

"That's good, my man; you tell your story capitally."

"De woman count de money plenty times, and tell all her fren's dat in about three or four months dey be able to marry in English church, an' dey make 'rangement for de lubly white dress, an' de blossoms she gwin to wear for de marrying.

"At dis time de man hab some trade in Freetown, an' been go down there for three or four days, an' when he come back he go down soon again, an' always gwin 'way like dat, but de woman 'spect nothing.

"One day, when he been come back, der big palaver in de house, an' much quarrel, an' all de neighbours run to see what de matter.

"Well, dey hyar dat de man hab tell de woman dat he been change his mind, an' no mean to marryen' her. Dat dey must half and half de money in de kettle, as he gwin to marry anudder woman, English fashion, at Freetown.

"Well, massa, dis bery bad palaver. Ain't all de person hyar bery poor? and ain't dis country weddin' rec'nised by de parents an' all de peoples?

"I nebber heard such ting, massa, as a man to leave n'a mudder of his picken jes' when dey hab save 'nuff to marry English fashion. In de country, under chief, if man do dis, de king flog him, an' sell him for slave one time (at once). But dis place under English, an' no 'nowledge country fashion like dat.

"But de man determined, an' de people all 'buse him, but no good; his friends stan' by him, 'cause de woman he gwin to marry in de town got shop, an doing fair business, an' he promise dem gran' weddin' next week.

"De woman like mad, an' go 'bout making much palaver against de bad man, and she buy n'a fetish charm to win him back again. But p'raps de man been buy stronger charm for de fetish not help her at all; of course she no sabbe dat, an' left all de money still in de ole kettle, for it sacred to de purpose. At last de man come back one day, an' say he gwin to take away his Sunday clothes one time (at once), an' dat dey better dwide de money. De woman fly in great rage, an' for fear ob making fight, de man go to bring his friends an' make palaver to arrange de matter, an' de woman been run to n'a gre-gre woman, an' tell her all about de affair, an' de money in de ole kettle.

"So de witch telled de woman to stand in de centre ob de floor, an' she make ring roun' her wid piece ob charcoal, which she den light, after talking witch palaver. She den 'gib de charcoal to de woman, and telled her to keep blowin' it an' not let it go out, an' to say between each blow " N'a ju-ju—n'a ju-ju—come cuss dis man;" while de witch say she gwin to get country medicine.

"After lilly while she come back an' den scatter medicine on de ring, an' after more witch palaver, she tell de girl hab no fear, but she can punish de man for true ("for true" means in this way, "without doubt.")

"De woman den get three or four friends, an' go back to de house, an' de man soon arrive with his friends, when dey proceed to make palaver. But all de talkee-talkee no good; de man no change his mind, and determined to throw over his country wife an' picken. At last de witch arrive with stick with two forks; some part got skin an' other part white (peeled), an' de woman tell her dat de man no 'gree to remain. So de ole witch telled all de other people to go away, an' dey all glad to go, an' den she made witch palaver, an' ask de man, 'If he determined for true to leave de woman an' picken an' take half de money?' An' he answer 'Yes.' Den she turn to de woman an' ask her 'What she want?' An' de woman answer, 'She no want nothing, but de man to stay.'

"So de witch den telled dem to produce de ole kettle, an' she draw ring round it, an' after some palaver—which nobody sabbe, she hit de kettle wid de stick, an' telled de man if he touch de ole kettle he nebber see de money, an' bad 'cuss go happen; an' den de witch go away.

" De friends come in again when dey see she gone, an' de man laugh an' tell dem all what she been do. De man been drinking rum all day, so he not frighten', so he kick de ole kettle out ob de ring, an' swing it open, and shake out de money; but instead, lot ob stones tumble on de ground. An' jus' den a laugh sound up in de roof; but dey look surprise', an' no can see nothing.

"So you see, massa," Davis continued, "de fetish woman witched de money away ——!"

"There's no doubt she did," I replied drily.

"Well, massa. Den de man begin to 'buse de woman, an' say 'he lock her up for thief,' 'cause by law all de money his; but she say nothing 'cept dat 'she not touch de money.' An' de friends telled de man to take his clothes as de tide rising, and dey are all gwin down to de marrying.

"So de woman watch him taking all his clothes, an' look at him straight wid de little picken in her arms, an' when he goin' out ob de door she say: 'Go—an' may n'a ju-ju nebber let you see de woman for whom you left me an' your lilly pickens."

CHAPTER XII.

ALLIGATORS AND WATERLOO.

"Is that the end of the story, Davis? What became of the man?"

"Well, massa, if you not tired, I gwin to tell you, but I'se a little thirsty. Well, massa," Davis continued, smacking his lips after his drink, "in de evening de man an' all his friends come down to de wharf to start for Freetown, when de tide was full up, as de weddin' to be next day. De men all dressed in de weddin' clothes, an' de man who gwin to get married hab on tail coat, an' boots, an' tall hat, an' gloves.

"An' music an' drum play de procession down to de wharf, where dey embark in big canoe, de marrying man sitting in de stern. Ebery man happy, 'cause dey been drinking rum all de day, an' dey laugh an' dey sing as de canoe shove off. De last ting de peeples see from de shore is de tall hat ob de man gwin to get married, an' de tail ob his coat hanging over de back ob de canoe.

"No man sabbe 'xactly how it happen, massa, but when de canoe 'bout half way down de creek, while dey is all laughing, de other men in de boat see de marrying man throw up his legs, an' wid' big holler he fall backwards into de water. De man who sat close to him say to de others, that he see alligator rise, catch hol' ob de coat-tails, an' pull him into de ribber. Well, massa, dey wait lilly minute, an' dey beat de water wid de paddles, to frighten de alligator away, but no good; de man nebber rise again, an' as he no answer when dey shout several times, dey pull on, for dey fear to turn de canoe round, an' dey all land at Rowesville.

"Well, next day some go down to town to tell de widder, an' some go back to report to de police at Waterloo, an' when dey go to de woman's house who he been left, dey find it shut; nobody seen her, nobody heard de picken cry in de night, dey cannot find de ole witch, an' tho' friends ask in Freetown, in Sherbro', in Regent, in ebery place in de colony, but nobody eber seen nor heard that they lib, an' no person seed them left Waterloo. After four or five days dey found de man's body close to de bank outside de creek, wid lilly bit eaten from de thigh an' from de left side, an' dat's all.

"Massa, you no tink it real alligator now, dɔ you? 'Cause it ju-ju alligator for sure which catch dat man, an' we'se all sure dat n'a witch hab turn de woman an' de pickens into ju-ju alligator, for to punish de man who runned away from her before all de peoples, against country fashion."

"Well, Davis, it's an extraordinary story, and the retribution was swift indeed."

"I no sabbe anyting about 'bution,' massa, but that alligator n'a ju-ju alligator, an' de woman witched it."

"But here we are at last," I said, as the boat, turning a bend of the creek, showed us Waterloo wharf lying before us.

"I beg you pardon, massa, before we land, but I like to say one ting particular. You been tell me lilly while back I 'nonsense, foolish fellow;' massa, dat bery bad word. You can call me anyting you like—idiot, jackass, n'a fool—damn fool—nigger; but, massa, nebber say me 'nonsense, foolish fellow' again; for to black man dat de worse curse you can ketch (find.) After all, massa, you can see dat n'a ju-ju lib in dis country."

"All right, Davis; I think you're a very sensible fellow, and you told your story in a most interesting way. As you have all had rather a long day, you shall have two bottles of rum to drink with your friends this evening."

"Thank you, massa; you bery good."

The boat was close in shore, and I was soon carried through the thick mud to terra firma, where a crowd had gathered to witness our arrival. But I looked in vain for my genial host, whom I felt sure would have come down to the landing-place to meet me. A police sergeant came up, and then explained that the manager was ill in bed with fever, and much regretted not being able to come down; so I followed him up the broad and clean street to my host's quarters.

Only a few days previously, during a hurried visit to Freetown, I had arranged to pay this visit, and on my arrival I found my friend in the throes of fever, tossing wearily from side to side, while the feverish skin and heightened colour showed too surely that it was a strong attack. Until my visit, there was not another white man within thirty miles, and many hours' journey. No medical advice at hand, beyond that of a native dresser; and yet, month after month, for several years, had my companion continued at this post—manager, magistrate, medical man, engineer, treasurer, and general factotum to the Government; but above all that, endeared and appreciated by the thriving inhabitants of the little town which he had improved and extended until, from an unimportant station it became one of considerable trade and prosperity.

Notwithstanding his illness, my arrival had not been forgotten; and with true hospitality a capital dinner had been prepared, which I was unfortunately unable to eat without the pleasurable companionship of my kind host. Next morning he was better, but quite unfit to show me round his interesting and extensive district; so I passed the day talking quietly with him, and postponed the trip into British Quiah, under his guidance, for a future occasion. I must start on the return journey before break of day, as I was due in Freetown about ten next day, and by hard pulling hoped to be able to manage it.

The "Wave" was repacked over night, and about an hour before daylight we were silently dropping down with the ebbing tide, a man on the bow with a lantern directing the course to be steered. It was nearly six, and broad daylight, when we emerged from the creek, the sun already shining with tropical strength. But what struck me with wonder and astonishment was that the mud-bank at the creek's mouth was alive with alligators, from the huge saurians, probably over a century old, to the baby alligator only a few feet long. Even the bank of the river was studded with them, lazily sprawling in the thick mud, wallowing like pigs in the sun. I searched in vain for ball cartridge, but I had expended them all, and I simply regarded with interest the doings of these leviathans of the creek.

"Massa, you nebber see nothing like dat before?"

"Never, my man."

"Well, massa, I beg you keep de dog quiet, for alligator lub dog better dan any ting else, an' I believe dey would upset lilly boat like dis for eat dog:" and when I remembered the encounter of but two days before, I thought such an act not impossible.

"Massa, I hope dat gre-gre not gwin to get we into trouble after all; too much alligator dere."

"I hope not, Davis; I think we'd better row a little faster."

The alligators appeared quite indifferent to the boat as it passed by the bank. Some of them were lazily crawling about, while others, with mouth wide open, seemed to be gazing at us.

"Why, Davis, there's a bird flying into the mouth of that one?"

"Yes, massa, I see de same ting plenty times up de Scarcies Ribber, when I work in de factory. Dat na tic-tac bird (a sic-sac plover); and if you watch 'um you see dat it eating insects which it catch inside the mouth." It certainly was eating some kind of grub as it flitted in and out of the great open mouth, and the operation appeared to be relished by the alligator; otherwise it would soon have settled the matter by abruptly closing its cavernous jaws. Again I searched in vain for but one round of ball ammunition, as a tempting shot presented itself, but without success. To fire fives or sixes at one of these brutes would have been as sensible as trying to take the Rock of Gibraltar with charges of peas.

"Massa!" said Davis, "n'a alligator wonderful ting. It can lib on de land, or in de sea, salt water, or fresh water—all de same. It born from egg like n'a chicken, an' de egg no bigger dan turkey egg. When he picken, every-ting can eat it: de bird eat 'um, de fish eat 'um, de snake can swallow 'um, an' yet dat lilly ting can grow big like dis, an' den eat all de tings which when he lilly, would hab eat himself. Jus' look at dat one der, what belly he got; an' look at all de shell an' mud on de back. Dat bery ole one, dat fellow, an' p'raps he been eat plenty poor black man. Massa! person nebber been see dead alligator, an' de peoples say dat when alligator die, de other ones bury 'um in de mud."

"Nonsense, my man!"

"For true, sah, you shoot alligator in de ribber, an' in course you can find him afterwards if you go look soon. But see de tousand an' tousand alligator dat lib, an' yet person nebber see dead one. Why? 'Cause de others bury 'um. When alligator meet dead alligator, he give 'um shove wid de nose towards de mud, den nudder one pass by an' gie 'um nudder shove, an' so on until dey get 'um in de mud, when dey walk over 'um until he covered up. Of course I no say person hab seen dat, but plenty black man talk so, an' as person nebber see dead alligator, I 'spects its true. De gall ob alligator deadly poison, an' make berry bad medicine; an' if chief catch person wid alligator gall in de house, dey kill him one time—dat de country law.

"In deep water, sah, de alligator not got much strength: he nebber bite person like shark, he drown 'um first. But in de shallow water de alligator bery strong. In deep water he half coward; but in shallow water he brave past everyting. Den dey can get der tail on de ground an' fight man, an' dat's de way dat alligator been ketch dat poor fellow de other morning."

"Yes, Davis, I should think alligators have nothing much to fear?"

"No, sah, n'a female hab lilly lizard which follow 'um about an' see where she lay de eggs, which he eat afterwards; but der be also one lilly fish which not afraid one bit ob alligator, an' when alligator see 'um coming, he shut his mouth, 'cause de fish can kill 'um."

"How does he do that, then?"

"Why, dis fish when he get inside alligator's mouth, he not quite like it, I s'pose, cause he open de fins, an' dey stick in de alligator's throat, an' I spects he hab bery bad time ob it, cause fish bone in de throat bery painful."

"Well, Davis, I'm quite interested about this little fish, and if you can prove your words, or get me one of them, I shall make you a dash (a present) of five shillings."

"Yes, massa, dese tings difficult to prove; but you ask Massa Budge next time you go to Waterloo. Plenty alligator lib in his district, an' he sabbe alligator palaver as much as any person. If I been tell you, sah, dat alligator can stand on his legs an' tail, an' fight man, you no b'lieve me prap's; but now you been seen it yourself, an' seen dat he no try to bite de man, but to throw him; you can get cross if person no can b'lieve you."

"Quite so, my man, I don't doubt what you say for a moment, and I have been most interested in your remarks. It would indeed be strange if the habits of these brutes were not pretty well known out here, with so many opportunities of seeing their ways."

By now we were heading down stream, and the alligators were far behind. The men bent willingly to their oars, in order to make as much way as they could with the ebb tide. The morning breeze was dead ahead, and it's a long steady pull of over thirty miles to Freetown. This they accomplished cheerfully and easily, without any further rest than occasionally changing the swing from the regular pull to what they call one and one, which means half-time rowing, or a pause between each stroke, and two and one, which is two regular strokes and the pause, and such other relaxation as was necessary to eat their frugal meal of rice and fish.

CHAPTER XIII.

A GENERAL DESCRIPTION OF FREETOWN.

FREETOWN contains many well-built houses in a good state of repair, though adjoining them there are a string of wooden shanties of varied shapes and sizes. In addition to the numerous well-to-do stores, many of them owned by natives, every African is possessed with the praiseworthy ambition of becoming a householder, and to accomplish this end he will live for years in the strictest economy, until the happy day arrives when he can blossom into a full-fledged landlord. To such an extent does this feeling prevail, that it is looked upon as a reproach for any native in a comparatively well-to-do position not to own one house at least.

The principal part of the town has therefore a clean and bright appearance, enhanced by the broadness of the streets, laid out on a regular plan. The appearance of these is much improved by a pathway of grass on each side, which affords a pleasing relief to the hard red earth, baked by the all-powerful sun.

There is a spacious fruit market close to the wharf. Here, in the early morning, may be seen a wealth of tropical fruit: bunches of plaintains and bananas, and large-sized pineapples, are jostled by green and brown-skinned oranges, while custard apples, avercardo pears (sometimes called alligator pears), melons, mangoes, guavas, limes, and other tropical fruits, besides a profusion of vegetables, are scattered about on the clean stalls. On most of these, small articles of personal vanity, and cheap mirrors and knives, are exposed in tempting juxta-position to the necessaries of life, and probably encourage the native servants to make a slight difference in their accounts of their purchases, in order to obtain whichever of these luxuries may excite their envy. Surely in no tower of Babel could more noise have been made than is heard here on a busy morning, while the gaudy print handkerchiefs and gowns of the women enliven the ever-changing scene. The services of the policeman on duty are seldom required to enforce order—everything is conducted good-humouredly. Yet the shouting, gesticulation, gleaming ivories, and glistening eyes, would lead a stranger to believe that a never-ending battle of arms and tongues is proceeding.

Close by the market-place the cathedral is situated, with its large windows—which unfortunately only open in one or two absurd places, and consequently let in too much garish light and far too little air. The structure is devoid of architectural beauty, and has been made still more hideous by repeated colourings of yellow-wash, instead of leaving the rough stone in its natural state. The interior is also devoid of architectural beauty, and was, until Governor Havelock's arrival, fitted with high shut-up pews. These he replaced by modern sloping benches, thus enabling the small amount of air that finds its way into the sacred building to circulate more freely, and getting rid of the dust and dirt which had accumulated in these old-fashioned pews for many years.

A more hideous set of lamps than those hanging in the aisles for use during the evening services could not have been designed. They resemble in shape the tawdry tin ones used at cheap fêtes and entertainments. A handsome lectern has recently been added—the gift of a poor black soldier, who, having no relations living, bequeathed his small savings for the purpose.

The cathedral is stated to have cost about seventy thousand pounds, and it is asserted that more than one fortune was made out of it before it was completed.

Near to it, and also facing the harbour, is the skeleton of a portentous building in red sandstone, temporarily roofed with zinc, while inside, iron beams and joists, and other paraphernalia of the building trade, almost indicate that the work of completion is still in progress. This is the Wilberforce Memorial, begun with much pomp many years ago, and intended to commemorate Africa's gratitude to that able philanthropist, to whom she owed so much. It was proposed that a public institution should be built, with library, reading, and lecture rooms adjoining. But the trustees, without taking the precaution of making sure of the funds first, commenced the building upon a scale which soon exhausted the considerable subcriptions in

A GENERAL DESCRIPTION OF FREETOWN. 149

hand, and they then found themselves compelled to abandon the undertaking after the walls and temporary roof had been erected.

On two occasions since, earnest appeals have been made to the natives to subscribe funds for the completion of the work ; but although these appeals have brought in several hundreds of pounds, they have demonstrated beyond question that the large sum necessary to finish and endow the trust are hardly likely to be forthcoming. Meanwhile this unfinished monument stands in all its incomplete ugliness, a blot upon the town, and a reproach to those who so hastily expended trust funds which must so far be considered as wasted.

But while it is an admitted impossibility that the original intention of the subscribers can be carried out, it is indeed a pity that the large sum already expended should be abandoned. As the building in its present state must soon decay, earnest endeavours should, I think, be made to remove this reflection upon the settlement and the natives, for which they are hardly to be blamed.

The present year is the Jubilee of Her Majesty's reign, and every part of the vast empire under her regal sway is putting forth its utmost strength to commemorate in some fitting manner the happy event. To my mind, this appears a most auspicious opportunity for remedying this undesirable state of affairs, and I have, therefore, fewer misgivings in submitting a plan by which much good might be done for Africa, and by which the money already expended can in part be regained.

The government offices of the colony are very badly situated, are in a tumble-down condition, and are quite unsuitable for the purpose, being nearly all in separate buildings, which necessitates much running to and fro between them, and multiplication of documents and accounts. Repetition is, therefore, unavoidable, especially as it is a rule of the Service that correspondence must pass through the Secretariat. In the same manner, all money must be paid into the Treasury, and consequently this separate system of offices causes increase of work, which could be easily avoided by judicious organisation.

I do not advocate that an amalgamation of departments under one head is advisable, as in such cases one of them becomes efficient at the expense of the others. But I do advocate that in a small colony it would be more economical and give increased efficiency by having as far as possible all the offices in one suitable building. In short, there is a decided inclination in the colonial service to consider each department as a separate office, instead of a part of a united system for the good government of the colony.

This Wilberforce Memorial is excellently situated and thoroughly suitable for government offices, and the Government, with its staff of workmen, and the command of convict labour also at hand, is in a position to turn this unsightly shell into a handsome set of public offices at a moderate expense. By such an arrangement a considerable annual saving could be made in the Treasury and Customs offices alone, since, owing to the offices being in separate buildings, two cashiers are required, and yet the cash has daily to be transferred to the Treasury, an operation involving labour, expense, and loss of time. If these departments were in the same building, much useless bookkeeping would be avoided, and one cashier would be sufficient. For the Customs having assessed their duties, the payee could be referred to the Treasury cashier, whose receipt would vouch for the payment. This one item would effect a saving of nearly four hundred pounds per annum.

But I have already stated that owing to the unhealthiness of the climate, officers are frequently compelled to personally superintend two and occasionally three separate departments. While they are in separate buildings, such an undertaking is extremely arduous, and necessitates much passing to and from, through a tropical sun, all of which would be avoided by the adoption of the plan of a central office.

My suggestion is, that the Government should take over this building at a fair valuation, or rent it at a fair rent, and the money thus received, together with that now on hand, should be invested to found scholarships for the education, in England, of two or more candidates selected among the natives after open competition. Her Majesty might be asked to graciously sanction that the Senior Scholarship be called the "Victoria Scholarship," in honour of her Jubilee, and of the centenary of the settlement (the first settlers having landed in August, 1787), and the second named the Wilberforce

A GENERAL DESCRIPTION OF FREETOWN. 153

Scholarship, in honour of that illustrious man, while if funds admitted it, a statue of that philanthropist would make a handsome additional commemoration of his noble work in behalf of this once enslaved race.

If Wilberforce were alive, surely such a scheme would commend itself to him even more than that which was proposed, but could not be carried through. If additional subscriptions be needed to carry out this suggestion, I am fully convinced that they would be forthcoming. Africans are a most generous race, and are ever ready to assist one another. So much is this the case that the wealthier ones frequently band together to pay for the education in England of any youths who to their minds have developed deserving capabilities. And from a keen study of their feelings and characteristics, I confidently assert that these scholarships would meet with hearty approval and support among them, and that any additional subscriptions necessary would be spontaneously offered for such a popular purpose.

The African naturally regards with pride every native who by ability and energy raises himself to a prominent position in the civilized world, and the good that would be accomplished by these scholarships must be too apparent to need more than passing mention. It was undoubtedly praiseworthy that an attempt should have been made to start a free library and institute and make it a commemorative work. But such an undertaking did not appeal to native feelings in the same way as these scholarships would. Besides this, the immense sum required to complete the building and endow it with sufficient funds to carry it on, ought certainly to have led the trustees to hesitate in beginning such a work until they felt quite positive that the necessary funds for its completion would be received.

I think the above suggestion may prove that the present unsatisfactory deadlock may yet be remedied, and Africa would still be commemorating, in a suitable and praiseworthy manner, her emancipation, her centenary, and her loyalty to our Sovereign Queen, of whom they are most dutiful subjects.

Proceeding past the fruit market, the next buildings of importance are the public hospital and gaol, both of which originally formed part of the commodious barracks in whose yards

A GENERAL DESCRIPTION OF FREETOWN. 155

thousands of slaves first received their liberty. The hospital contains nearly a hundred beds, and urgent cases are always admitted, while outdoor relief is granted daily to those requiring it, the medicines being given gratis to the poor, and in other cases charged at cost price. A class of native students receive instruction from the colonial surgeon, and if apt, are promoted to district dispensaries, where with made-up medicines, and concise directions how to act in specific cases, their services are of value to the poorer Africans.

Over a disused gateway are two pieces of iron chain, which have a somewhat harmless appearance; but it frequently occurred to me whether the poor wretch from whom these shackles were struck off remembered the day when, stiff and starving, he received his liberty, and perhaps his life, after many vicissitudes.

Close by, over a high wall, a huge fan-like windmill is grinding its useless way with well-greased throbs. This is the treadmill of the prison, and eight men, stripped to their loins, and perspiring from the result of such labour, are doing their ten minutes on, to cause that revolving shutter to spin round. Here nearly three hundred men are incarcerated for various offences, many of them being habitual offenders, theft being a common crime in the colony. The prison is one difficult to manage, the building being so small that no solitary system can be carried out; and what is still more disadvantageous, through want of accommodation, batches of prisoners have to occupy the same cell, while the prison yard is so littered with benches, tables, and kitchen buildings that it is impossible to maintain anything beyond the merest show of discipline.

The youth incarcerated for his first offence, probably a minor one, is drafted into the same gang as the hardened convict. The murderer, and the repeatedly-convicted thief, mix not only with those doing penance for less serious offences, but with untried men who are compelled to occupy the same yard until the sessions come which decide their fate. It is not surprising therefore that the Africans beyond the walls look upon the man awaiting trial in the same light as though he had been convicted.

In a separate building, which forms part of the gaoler's quarters, the political prisoners are confined. Here sits one who has been incarcerated for several years for fomenting native disturbances and engaging in continuous wars. He is spelling out from his beloved Koran to others squatting round, and expresses himself very grateful for this recently granted indulgence. He is at present unaware that the Secretary of State has directed his release, when he will gladly return to his people, who will receive him with increased respect, while the severe lesson he has had will make him lead a more cautious and less pugnacious life.

Beyond the gaol, and facing the bay is the old Government House, in which the chequered career of the colony's infancy and growth was planned. The building is now used as a Grammar School, and is perhaps the best conducted school on the West Coast. In it natives are educated as in a high-class school at home, and on its forms many can be found quite up to the Standard educational tests of the Oxford and Cambridge local exams.

From the water's edge, the land rises by a steep incline through the town, and about half a mile from the shore lies Government House on a made mound dignified by the name of Fort Thornton. But as a few yards higher up it is completely commanded by the rising ground, its defensive powers are very limited. Above it, the saluting battery, fringed round with green bushes, answers back the courteous salutes of the foreign men-of-war visiting the station; while higher up the hill are the barracks occupied by the West India Regiment for the time being stationed in the colony. There are now but two of these regiments, the others having been disbanded; and they serve alternately between the West Indies and the West Coast of Africa. The dress of the men is an extremely picturesque one, and is stated to have been designed by Her Majesty. The officers wear the ordinary uniform of the Line. These regiments are nearly always in detachments, both in the West Indies and on the coast, consequently they have little opportunity for battalion drill and are therefore much behind the British soldier in smartness and precision. As marksmen they invariably occupy the unenviable position of being the worst in the service, and no amount of "position" and "aiming drills" seems to have any effect in making them shoot straight. When the Snider was discarded for the Martini, the men indulged in much grumbling (at which they are adepts) on account of the recoil, and in one instance a soldier absolutely refused to use his rifle at all, with the result that after suffering the usual punishments for disobedience, it was found advisable to grant the man his discharge. The officers are generally a nice set of fellows, but there are not nearly enough of them to a battalion. Owing to the unhealthiness of the climates in which they serve, many are constantly on sick leave and furlough, and junior lieutenants are frequently compelled to take charge of companies, which is hardly a fair proceeding with the risks of loss that company officers have to suffer. The number of captains should certainly be increased, and if promotion is brisk in these regiments, it must be remembered that spending one's life between the West Coast of Africa and the West Indies is not the most enjoyable existence that one would select; therefore to retain good men among them, such extra inducements of quick promotion should be held out.

Oddly enough, the two regiments rather dislike one another, and if you happen to say anything to a fellow in the 1st West about the 2nd, he snorts and speaks of it with ineffable disdain, while his brother officer in the 2nd will say, "Poor chap, I don't envy him being in that regiment, I can tell you—rum lot the 1st."

The men are much given to hymn-singing and ladies, and owing to their Don Juan propensities and jealousies, the razor is not allowed to form part of their kit, as false vows lead to serious rows among them. Like Africans—for they are the descendants of manumitted bondsmen—they sleep with a density almost equivalent to a trance, and when a negro is once well off to sleep he seems impervious to noise, while an occasional blow or two makes little difference. A remarkable instance of this occurred at the officers' mess. The store-room beneath is built on huge iron joists, and one of the mess waiters slept in this room as a sort of guard. One night the officers were disturbed by a loud noise which shook the building. Lamps were soon lighted, and it was discovered that one of these iron joists had fallen in the store-room, while the messman slept on unaware of the narrow escape he had had. When interrogated about it next day, after much confusion he said "he thought he had heard a rat, but wasn't sure." Inasmuch as the noise had disturbed

M

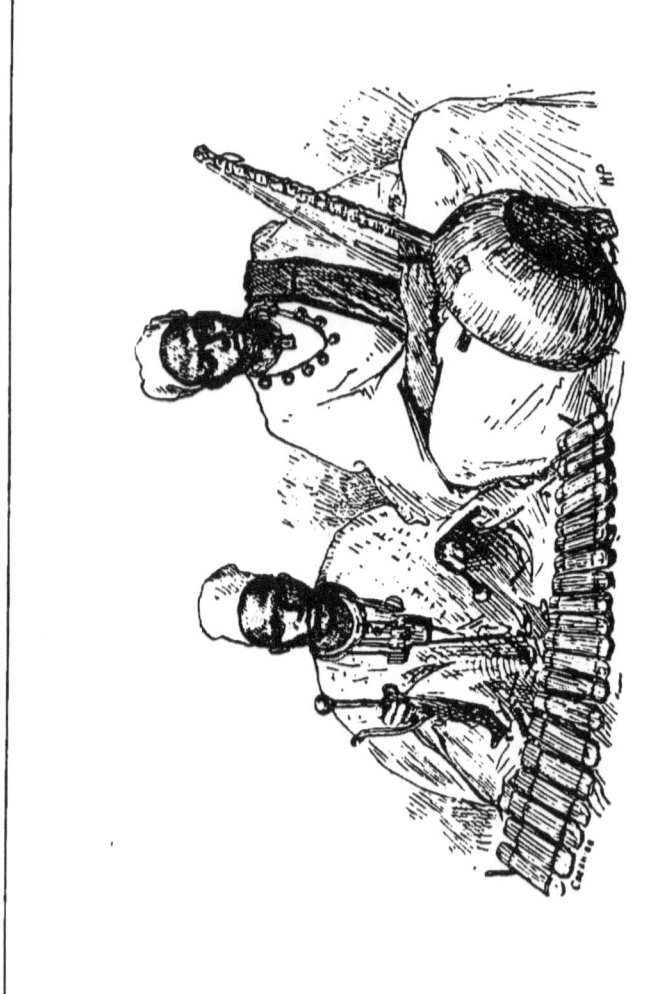

MANDINGO MUSICIANS.

the whole of the officers, this instance will exemplify how soundly negroes sleep, and how efficiently this particular African's presence protected the store from thieves.

There are numerous churches and chapels in the colony, and almost every form of dissent is represented. As these different sects do not love one another, Christianity has not produced the same effect upon the pagan mind as would have been the case had there been only one form of Christian worship represented. One wily old Mahomedan who was approached by a dissenting minister took the greatest interest in listening to his remarks, though he did not like the "Trinity," especially the "Ghost" part of it. He, however, put a stop to all attempts at his further conversion, by telling the minister that he looked upon the white men as cleverer than the poor black ones; and that when they had settled among themselves which was the best form of worship, if he came back to him, he would then compare it with his doctrine, that there is only one Allah, and Mahomed was his prophet.

The Christianised natives are much given to hymn-singing and harmonium-playing, and in almost every house devotional exercise is daily conducted. Christianity has undoubtedly a firm hold over the Sierra Leonians, and I have frequently heard impromptu sermons preached by poor shoeless men who were barely able to read the Scriptures, of a very high order. And what is still more praiseworthy, they are able to quote chapter and verse in support of their appealing addresses.

Much has been written and said against the morals of the natives, and there is little doubt civilized notions of propriety are anything but strictly regarded. Concubinage and illegitimacy are not looked upon as gross vices, to be hidden from the respectable world. Yet when it is remembered that with the poor and ignorant these crimes are not crimes at all, but recognised as local customs, the percentage is very largely reduced. Among others, the Old Testament is often quoted in support of such habits; and an African, with that keenness of argument which they possess in such an eminent degree, assured me that he looked upon Europeans as fulfilling the New Testament of the world, and the Africans as having been specially preserved to continue in the ways of the Old Testament;

thus proving to the world at large the truth of the Bible. It must be remembered also that the unhealthiness of the climate prevents that softening influence of comparison which would be gained if it were possible for English ladies to live in the country.

The only other buildings of importance are the Government offices, and they are devoid of architectural beauty, and ill-fitted for the purpose. There is also a college affiliated with the Durham University, situated at Fourah Bay, which is a short distance from Freetown, but this has of late years dropped down to a very low ebb, despite the fact that the headmaster is generally a European.

CHAPTER XIV.

THE TRADE OF THE COLONY.

THE sparseness of population of the surrounding country, which precluded the settlement fulfilling the hopes of the Sierra Leone Company, the absence of those vast incentives to trade, good roads and navigable rivers, the inertness of the few tribes that exist in the neighbourhood, hardly advanced, if advanced at all, one step in civilization since the day when the English settlers first landed, the perpetual internecine wars, which frequently stop all trade, and the unhealthiness of the station, have prevented Sierra Leone making that progress in trade, and in the development of the resources which undoubtedly lie dormant on its fever-stricken shores.

As a consequence, the exports of the colony are dependent more upon the bounteous provision of nature than upon any human aid; and rich crops are only to be gathered after the impoverished ground has recouped itself by natural causes. The native plan is simply to reap everything year after year, while it pays to do so; but when the quality of the produce has so deteriorated through want of manure as to make it worthless, then they leave it to regain its vigour by the aid of nature. The ground is capable of producing almost any tropical product, but none are planted. There are miles of low-lying sandy earth, almost inviting cocoa-nuts to plant themselves, yet they remain unplanted year after year. Rice would grow in thousands of acres that lie fallow, unless the rank grass may be considered of any value. It has been proved that coffee thrives excellently, but the people are too inert to pay the necessary attention to it. But it is the same with many other valuable plants, all of which would thrive, none of which are planted.

The trade of the settlement may be divided into two broad divisions: that of the settlement proper, or trade within British jurisdiction; and the trade without the settlement, but controlled within it, and for which it forms the bonded warehouse. In the colony the stores generally carry on both a wholesale and retail trade, either for cash or in exchange for the produce that is brought down from the interior. The wholesale transactions in this way are diminishing, as the natives find they obtain better equivalents in the stores outside jurisdiction, the goods in them having been transhipped in bond. The retail business is rapidly falling into the hands of the natives, who with but small capital, and sometimes on credit only, open a mere box of a shop to begin with, and by business attention and cheap prices make a competence where a white trader would starve.

The instinct for trade seems to be inherent among them; from the young child hawking cakes or tobacco about the streets, to the grown-up man or woman with basket or little shanty, all are engaged in the task of selling their wares. Pen can hardly describe the condition of streets, such as Kissy Street and Kroo Town Road, every house a shop, and every shop a bazaar, while the footway is lined on both sides with squatting vendors of cooked or uncooked provisions. The jostling crowd is full of others perambulating to and fro, uttering shrill cries of the nature, the price, and the quality of their wares. Of a verity, the child seems to be a man almost from his birth, and engaged in the battle of earning a livelihood, while, strange to say, as soon as he has passed the tender years, then he becomes a child again, idling, laughing, and enjoying the day, as if there was no morrow —happy, unconscious, uncaring for the days to come, feeling no misgivings as to whether they will be days of plenty or of scarceness, of good provisions or of semi-starvation.

The importations consist of tobacco, hardware goods, gunpowder, guns—certainly made from disused or condemned gas pipes, vast quantities of Manchester goods, and Birmingham wares, and the vilest compound of trade spirits made expressly for the trade at Hamburg. The exports are ginger, ground nuts, india rubber, copra, beniseed palm oil and palm kernels, gold, ivory, hides, and wild animals. Of late years a lucrative trade has grown up with the Gambia in Kola nuts, a trade which is entirely in the hands of the natives. The kola nut is not unlike the vegetable ivory nut in appearance, and of these and chew-sticks the natives are specially fond. These nuts are quite white inside, and moderately hard. Chewing them produces an intensely acid taste in the mouth, accompanied by a peculiar dryness, and yet not robbing the mouth of its secretions. Why the natives are so fond of them, it is difficult to imagine. The taste is undoubtedly disagreeable, though owing to their astringent qualities, they are supposed to have the power of allaying hunger. Whether this is anything more than the working of the gastric juices which may be accomplished by chewing any slightly bitter substance is very doubtful. It is not, however, on this ground that the natives are always eating the nut, for its price is about threepence, and for that sum an African can obtain enough rice and bungay (rotten fish) to last for the day. The natives like to have something always in their mouth, and if they cannot afford the kola nuts, they are satisfied with the ordinary chew-stick, which they will save up from day to day in the same way that a sailor will his quid of tobacco.

The kola nut possesses one peculiarity: a glass of water taken with it has an intensely agreeable and pure taste, appearing to dwell in the throat and descending slowly with a pleasing coolness probably due to the relief it gives to the roughened and contracted palate. These nuts have been turned into a patent medicine, and in that form they may doubtless assist digestion in those who take insufficient exercise, or whose digestion may have been weakened through other causes.

The colony enjoys an immunity from taxation, the only dues being on certain of the imports and spirits. In order to trade without paying these, most of the large firms have factories scattered up the adjacent rivers above the northern boundaries of the settlement, which are kept supplied from the bonded warehouses, thus escaping the import duties. Numbers of canoes and boats, and a few steam launches, are engaged in keeping these out-stations supplied and in returning with the produce received in exchange. By keeping the largest stock of goods within the colony, the merchants minimize the risks they are liable to sustain owing to these out-stations being beyond the limits of British jurisdiction, and there devoid of protection.

The trade in these out-stations is mostly carried on by the system of exchange, an opportunity for cash transactions rarely occurring. But the former gives the trader the double profit—that on the goods sold and also the profit that he will receive for the produce in the English market. The natives are keenly alive to the relative value of their produce, and long practice, competition, and dearly-bought experience have made them good business men, and they soon discover whether there is any rise or fall in the market prices.

In one of my expeditions in the "Wave" I was much interested in the way business is conducted in these outside factories. Several large canoes laden with produce had turned the bend of the river and approached the wharf with much tum-tumming and singing, and my host went outside to receive them.

"Hah! Alimani, I am glad to see you again—you well, eh? Plenty good trade, I hope."

"Not bery much dis time, tings bery scarce," replied the chief. As the natives clamber up the wharf I am introduced as " n'a Government Secretary," and we exchanged friendly salutations.

White trader (keenly): "Well, Alimani, you want to sit down and have a blow, or you like to have some chop one time—or begin trade now?" This, in ordinary English, meant, Will you rest a while, or have something to eat at once, or trade first? "Chop" is not a bad word for food, and derives its origin in "Pidgin English" from "palm oil chop," in which pieces of chopped pork and fowl, mixed up with oil and rice, make the above well-known but greasy dish.

The Alimani desired to begin trading at once.

Trader: "Hah, jus' so—trade first, that's good. Well, let your boys land the produce on the wharf, and we'll have a drink, eh?"

Alimani: "No hurry for unload yet. Want to see de tings in de store first. Cause if I no likee, I can go down to de French factory."

This is a hint that prices must be reasonable, and shows that the visitor is well up to the work before him, and too old a bird to be caught by chaff. We therefore adjourned to the store, where bale after bale was examined—white shirting, blue baft, coloured handkerchiefs, knives by the dozen, showily made wellington boots with painted uppers and tassels, flint-lock guns with painted stocks, very tinny looking-glasses, giving a gastly hue even to a negro countenance; tall hats, kegs of gunpowder, rum in casks and demijohns, square-faced bottles of geneva in green cases containing a dozen each, innumerable trinkets, both of glass and coral: all are critically examined by the natives, who indulge in shrill " Hies!" as anything strikes their fancy or excites their surprise. The headmen are much less demonstrative, but bent on doing the best they can, frequently asking how many for a " bar," which is the unit of calculation in their dealings. Thus a certain number of coloured handkerchiefs go to a bar, and the same with spirits, tobacco, and trinkets—they all have their equivalent in "bars."

While the things are being examined, the white trader endeavoured to find out what the chief had. " Much rubber dis time, Alimani?" " No, bery little—rubber dear now." Presently a portion of the cargo is landed, and before anything more was produced, the bargaining for this must be completed.

" Well, chief, what do you want for these kernels?" The native made his demand, and the haggling began until the matter was settled, when they both declared that they were losers by the transaction. As the bartering continued, the natives became more exacting, and certainly appeared to obtain a very fair equivalent for their produce.

In order to quicken trade, a glass of rum was next given to each of the under-men, while the white trader invited the Alimani and myself to have a drink with him, for which purpose we adjourned to his private office. Here he became very friendly with the native, and in a series of complimentary terms informed me that the Alimani is well diposed towards the English.

"Now, chief, we'll have some good champagne, eh?" And I certainly observed a perceptible wink in the off-eye as he looked at me.

"Boy—open a bottle champagne; those large one's with gold paper: you sabbe?" "Yes, sah," came back the reply. Champagne glasses were produced, and after an explosive pop, they were filled with the sparkling wine. Having clinked glasses, as we lifted them up I again noticed that my host was eyeing me inquisitively, while his eye again went through a series of winks. Without knowing exactly why, I winked spasmodically in return.

White trader: "Now, chief, here's to good

friendship and business "—and we take the first gulp.

"Why, bless me," I cried, "this is ——"

"Very good, isn't it?" hastily interrupted my friend, while his eye began again to dislocate itself in an alarming manner. So I feebly answered, "Oh yes, very;" my host, turning to native, "Very good, eh, chief?"

Chief, "Yes: no bad drink." And I again dubiously said, "Oh yes, very good."

White trader, growing bolder: "Yes, chief, I'm glad you like it," refilling his glass. "Have another glass; it's very good champagne, isn't it? I can sell ——"

Alimani: "Well, I nebber said it champagne, but it's not bad cider"—and I turned away and examined some of the prints about the room, so as to avoid laughing right out at my friend's well-earned discomfiture.

"Quite right, chief, quite right; it's very good champagne cider, but we call it champagne for short name, you know."

In the evening, after the canoes had left, we laughed heartily over the occurrence as my host exclaimed, "Who would have expected the old beggar would have known the difference?"

Life in these out-stations is not an enviable one. Sometimes months pass by without the society of a single person with whom to converse. No roads for exercise, no sport, no one to converse with but the natives employed in the factory, and the constant anxiety, not only for health but for the peacefulness of the natives, who are ever ready to engage in internecine wars, which stop all trade and threaten the loss of the factory.

Imagine, too, the muddy river, daily at low tide giving forth its deadly smell, while the eye wanders up and down its monotonous course, with nothing but the unvarying mangrove bush, teeming with insect life which keeps up a ceaseless buzz throughout the day. After dark, the voracious mosquito drives one to take shelter, at an early hour, behind the netting of the bed, while over the land, that dull, dank, mist rises, carrying death in its insidious folds and forming a funeral pall, until the heat of the morning sun chases it gradually away.

CHAPTER XV.

ANNEXATIONS AND CUSTOMS.

THE original settlement under the Crown included the peninsula of Sierra Leone only, for though Sir Charles Turner, in 1826, extended the boundary as far south as the Boom River, the claim was evidently allowed to lapse, since it was deemed advisable in the re-annexation of that territory (1884) to enter into fresh treaties with the ceding chiefs. When the palaver at which this treaty was signed was held, the stump of the old cotton tree was pointed out with pride by the natives as the one that had been destroyed by Sir Charles Turner; and, probably, during the intervening period (1826—1884) the site had not been visited by a single white person.

In 1862 a large tract of country, called Sherbro', which lies to the south of the original

A WAR-BOY WITH FETISH.

settlement, was surrendered by treaty, and has proved extremely valuable to the prosperity of the colony, being rich in African produce, and possessing several rivers sufficiently navigable to assist its development. The district is under the management of a Civil Commandant, but being very large and scattered, it is impossible to keep the natives in hand, and constant local squabbles, frequently on territory within our jurisdiction, not only hamper trade, but result in lawlessness and bloodshed.

In 1879 it was deemed politic to extend the colony towards the north, in order to keep possession of its trade, as the French had been pushing south, and had acquired stations at Mellacourie, and at Binty, which are in close proximity to Sierra Leone. Consequently, Sir Samuel Rowe took possession of a small island, called Kakonkeh, at the mouth of the Great Scarcies River. This not only protects British interests in the north of the settlement, but gives it control of the magnificent waterway, and the trade passing to the important Mahomedan centres to which it leads. This was a masterly move on the part of the Governor, and was carried out much to the astonishment of the warlike Foulahs, who by no means relished the unexpected control to which they suddenly found themselves subjected, notwithstanding all their previous protestations of loyalty and goodwill. At first it appeared that troubles would arise from this step, for the Foulahs assembled in thousands, with the intention of driving the few policemen from the island, and thus vindicating their claim to a free water-way to the interior.

However, Sir Samuel Rowe was equal to the occasion, and promptly ascended the river with a company of the 2nd West and a few policemen, and boldly landed at the native town in the midst of the gathering hordes. No more fearless action has ever been performed than this. Already the news of the approach of the Governor and his few men had been received, and the war drums were beating as they landed, while the Foulahs, in their long white robes, were rushing from all parts with their wild cry of "Allah-il-Allah," as they worked themselves into fanatical fury for the coming conflict. There could hardly have been less than five thousand of them, well armed, surrounding the little band of soldiers and police, with their few officers, as they forced their way through the threatening throng—led by the stalwart Governor—to the chief's house. This handful of men were kept together with loaded arms, back to back, while Sir Samuel Rowe coolly sat down among the astonished chiefs and started a palaver. Here the Governor's invaluable knowledge of African character stood him in good stead, and his tact and fearlessness, while he held the ever necessary palaver, in which he beat the natives in their own arguments, undoubtedly saved the lives of himself and his small escort on this most ticklish occasion.

In 1884 the colony was extended in the south until its borders were conterminous with the boundaries of the Republic of Liberia; and the settlement now possesses an uninterrupted seaboard from the Great Scarcies, on the north, to the Mannah River, on the south; a definite boundary, which should, in times to come, assist the development of the settlement, as law and order gradually take the place of the bloody internecine squabbles that have been hitherto so disastrous to advancement.

As the unhealthiness of the climate prevents any large increase of European population, it is essential that every means should be adopted to civilize the natives, since the future of the settlement must, to a very large extent, be dependent upon them. Unless means be found for producing this result, the colony must continue, century after century, in its present paradoxical condition of barbaric-civilization. It therefore becomes imperative that increased facilities for education should be adopted, and there is little doubt that a marked improvement would take place in a comparatively short time. Governor Havelock, with that discernment for which he is so justly appreciated, perceived this fact, and not only worked hard in establishing schools in districts where education had previously been unknown, but took every opportunity of promoting deserving natives when they were competent and efficient.

But much more requires to be done in this way. The whole settlement should be mapped out into educational districts, and these districts placed under native inspectors. In each district free schools ought to be established in all the towns and large villages, under native masters and mistresses. These should be constantly visited by the district inspector, while the English superintendent would supervise the whole. Such a plan, if properly organised, would cost very little, as native teachers are easily obtainable at very modest wages.

At present the whole of the West Coast of Africa, from Sierra Leone to the Gold Coast, is under the charge of one Superintendent of Education, and much of his time is necessarily taken up in travelling along this lengthy seaboard. There is nothing personally disparaging in saying that little good can be effected under such a system, while the funds for educational purposes are totally inadequate, when it has been over and over again demonstrated that the improvement of the colony depends upon the advancement of the natives.

None of the dialects spoken among the various native tribes outside the settlement have written signs, excepting the Foulahs, and other Arabic-speaking tribes, while in the settlement proper " Pidgin English " is nearly universal. If recent annexations are omitted, I doubt if there is a single village in the settlement where "Pidgin English " is not understood, and such a fact very much facilitates the introduction of English education.

The natives still retain their old superstitions

and customs, and even those among them who have been sent to England for education, cannot shake off their absolute belief in spirits and charms, both for good and for evil. It is extremely difficult to describe the origin of some of their superstitions, for anything may be a gre-gre or fetish. Thunder, lightning, rain, an eclipse, drought, torrents, waterspouts, a landslip, wild animals, any illness—in fact all forms of destruction, either by accident or disease, are associated with superstition, and the charms against them vary at the absolute will of the medicine men and witches among the pagans; while, among the Mahomedans, certain texts of the Koran, if blessed by the proper medicine man, possess the same curing or preventing power. Even the failure of the witches (for the term is used among them for both sexes) only strengthens the belief of the people, and thus enables the medicine folks to continue practising upon the credulity of the people.

Beyond jurisdiction, sacrifices and slaughter are still carried on. Trials by ordeal, of both fire and poison, are frequent. Unfaithfulness of wives, or concubines, affords opportunity for a special medicine man detector, and he will be feasted with plenty to-day, and dash out the wretched woman's brains on the morrow, under the pretended discovery of marital sin. Secret cannibalism is also prevalent, though the native punishment for this custom is death, and in the Mendi mission (an American society) they possess the skin of a large leopard, with iron claws, which had once been the property of a man who, under this guise, satisfied his horrible craving. The medicine men themselves are frequently guilty of mysterious crimes, which they afterwards charge against innocent victims, so as to retain or increase their reputation as seers.

To be a witch, one must have taken human life or be credited with some supernatural power over the unknown and mysterious. To be a successful medicine man, one must possess quick powers of penetration, decision, and a knowledge of subtle vegetable poisons, and their specifics, which enables him to kill one and cure another, while to onlookers both have taken the same poison. The belief of both educated and ignorant in the ability of these medicine folks is unshaken, and they are consulted for everything and by everybody. The young lover will solicit a gre-gre to make his suit successful ; the girl will ask for one that she may not be jilted ; she will again ask for one for the safe birth of her child, for the sex she wishes, and, above all, that it should not be stillborn. Such is a general description of West African witchery, but there are certain defined superstitions which may be interesting.

One day the office messenger came and asked for leave of absence. His face was in agony, and he pointed to his arm, which he said had been witched by a woman. So much did he believe it himself that he had applied to the police magistrate for a summons, though he admitted that he had never seen the woman. He also seemed powerless to raise his arm. The colonial surgeon soon cured this case by a powerful shock from an electric battery. Under its effects the arm recovered instantaneously, while the fellow turned livid with fright at this new kind of cure, as he capered at the end of the handles which he could not easily drop. His own explanation afterwards was that "he nebber sabbe such medicine which make him jump in ebery part, though he tried to stand still."

Two women walking on a road will not separate if they can possibly help it, to allow a man to pass between them. Such an act (I am afraid, coupled with their slackness of morals) would, to their ideas, result in their becoming mothers. Two men passing between them they fancy, would, in certain circumstances, cause twins, and to prevent such a catastrophe they will turn and run away. Women with child separate themselves from their husbands, from that time until the child is weaned. This custom is universal, and is believed in thoroughly by well educated natives. So ingrained is this superstition, that the wife not only sanctions the husband breaking his vows, but in many instances will allow another woman to live in the same house with the husband and herself. This peculiar superstition arises from a firm belief that the unborn or nourished child would not only be unhealthy, but unlucky, in consequence.

Certain parts of the body of a still-born child are much sought after for medicines and gre-gres, and graves are desecrated for the purpose of obtaining the bodies of girls of tender age who die under peculiar conditions. Failing a supply of these disgusting medicines, the witch doctor will manufacture substitutes from pigs. Love philtres can always be obtained, and as they take the form of noxious and vicious incentives, and the woman or man, as the case may be, is advised to closely watch the result, they are frequently effective in the manner desired.

Growing crops are protected from thieves by fetish charms hung upon a branch of a tree in a conspicuous place. The gre-gre may be only a shell or a few loosely strung bones, or a neck of a bottle, sometimes a rudely-drawn coffin, but as they have all been cursed to do harm to evil-doers they serve their purpose. The head of the iguano (a species of large lizard) is supposed to be a sure specific against certain complaints in children, and I always gave the head to my boatmen for their children whenever I shot one of them.

Among the polygamic tribes there exists a cruel custom called Bundoo, which is the excision of parts of a female with a view of securing her chastity. This rite, a rite of circumcision among females, is performed in villages set apart for the purpose by old women, to whom parents send their daughters when they are between ten and twelve years of age, and many die under the horrible operation.

Then there is the weird and mystic "Porrah," a sort of barbarous Freemasonry existing among the pagan tribes. The meetings are held at night-time in the bush, the leaves of which are plaited in some mystic way, which is detected by the natives, who will never enter inside the mystic ring of bush so guarded. No man will pass within some distance of this, even in the daytime, without whistling or making a noise to notify that he is in the neighbourhood. While the "Porrah" boys are out at night, holding their meetings, which are generally on moonlight nights, women will not leave their houses at all. The "Porrah" sentries encircling the deep shadowed grove, will keep up a weird chanting shout to warn all people away. None could pass through these tylers of this Society without the sign; to attempt such a thing would be instant death, nor would the murder ever be traced.

Any person passing by, even at a distance, must give warning of his approach and obey the unknown voice commanding him to stop or return, otherwise from some low bush a form would suddenly rise, there would be a dull shadow across the dark ground, and a headless corpse would be secretly buried unknown to the outer world. The origin and design of this secret Society has never been traced. It is evidently of great antiquity, and bears a strange resemblance to the weird meetings of the Druids of early British history, whose worship was also carried on mid the deep glades of the forests, and also consisted of sacrifices, both human and of other animals and birds, on stated occasions. To "Porrah" agency the frequent disappearance of innocent girls must be ascribed. Their bodies are sometimes found afterwards with certain parts removed. But the history of these sacrifices can only be imagined, for as a Society among a pagan and superstitious people, its laws and customs are inviolate and untraceable.

In it there are different grades of initiation, and those not admitted into the inner ring know nothing of the incantations there carried on. For hours no voices will be heard, and the rites are then conducted by mysterious signs until the worship of the "Porrah" Devil becomes a hideous revelry on which the sombre light of the moon casts its fitful shadows. This will be followed and extended from the inner ring gradually to the outer folds, where all will combine in a wild dance, as though a set of demons from another world had suddenly arisen. The "Porrah" Society has hold of thousands of devotees, and probably consists in the worship of the God of goodness and the propitiation of the God of evil, by the presentation of certain forms of innocent blood after many rites. The grave disadvantage of such an order lies in the superstitious belief in the power of evil, and the necessity for conciliating the demon representing it.

Passing up the river one bright moonlit night, I heard the weird shouts of the "Porrah" boys warning strangers to keep away. The men told me that a "Porrah" palaver was being held, and that we must not ascend much further unless permitted to do so. Presently one of the men gave a warning shout, to notify that we were passing, and to my imagination the answering cry appeared longer and shriller and was taken up from many parts of the river's bank. The men continued shouting from the boat, and at last the cry of the "Porrah" changed in tone and ended off differently. After this change nothing would persuade the men to proceed further, and the boat was taken over to the far shore and anchored, while the shouts of the sentinels, none of whom were visible, created a weird feeling in me, not diminished by the superstitious behaviour of the men who, with bated breath, continued talking among themselves.

CHAPTER XVI.

A SAD CASE, AND NATIVE OATHS.

AT the office one morning I received an urgent request from the colonial surgeon to attend, if possible, at once, and take down the deposition of a girl who had been stabbed. When I arrived at the hospital, the nurse conducted me to the bedside of a young Timaneh girl, probably about fifteen years of age. She was an exceedingly pretty specimen of a negro girl, and her ruddy brown skin of satin-like appearance set off a figure budding into early womanhood, while her face was one of intelligent expression, and little betokened her rapidly approaching death.

In reply to my inquiry the nurse told me that she had been brought in from a small town near Waterloo but a few days before, and had been stabbed in three places by her husband, to whom she was married country fashion. He had seen another man leaving his rude hut, who had run away on seeing him, and acting upon the impulse of jealous exasperation, he had ruthlessly plunged a long knife into the unfortunate girl, and then escaped into the bush. " She no sabbe, sah, that she cannot lib," the nurse added ; and as the girl did not know a word of English, the nurse interpreted into Timaneh the painful words I had to impart.

In answer to my interpreter the girl said her name was "Tidankie" (what a pretty name), and a heavy lump rose in my throat as I told the nurse to explain to "Tidankie" that she was on the point of death, and that what she was going to say to me must be under the absolute knowledge and belief that she could not recover.

The dying girl was a heathen, or as the nurse said, " She no sabbe look palaver, sah," and consequently could not be sworn on the Bible. So two pieces of iron were produced, one a part of an old rake, and the other a large rusty nail —for any iron will do. These I placed in " Tidankie's " dying hands, and she feebly knocked them together in musical time as she repeated the following Timaneh oath after me, in a soft voice :

" Sahnje ! sahnje ! sahnje ! Pah-tol !
Meneh ! Meneh ! tenteneh,
Ampah meneh, dah bakie annoi,
Bapeh, e gabakie era-ameh,
Bapeh, e tari meh,
E tari, antokoh mu,
Bapeh, e barkah robileh—e tar ambil,
Olongah tar anque o' bep me !
Bapeh e Kor !—Vocanhe e tar ! –obokeh !
Orbanah or ngar meh,
Bapeh, e gbapeh rocoompeh, e corten !
Amarroh or markalleh,—tar e fulreh,
Bapeh meh, e deh anak car affatee,
E, darreh dai, pah rayameh robarri,
Ornoh alli ar yokah
Tar Correh car me
Boyah gberoh, meneh e fi
Bapeh e pareh ayameh fong faing.
Loutah !"

This oath is extremely musical, and repeated with inflections and tappings of the iron with emphasis on the sentences. Its translation is as follows :

"Of a truth, truth, truth Pah Medicine
I, I, of a truth,
The words I am going to talk,
If I talk or answer lies !
If you leave me,
You leave your fowl.
If I go in a canoe let it sink,
And let alligator catch me ;
If I go into the bush,
Let big snake bite me;
If I climb a tree for palm oil or palm wine,
Let me fall down ;
If I eat rice cooked in a pot
After talking lies in this case,
Or if I eat cassada,*
Let my belly swell and let me die ;
But, if I speak the truth,
Let me be free from these curses,
Amen !"

---

* There is a poisonous cassada.

"Tidankie" then kissed the two irons, and her oath was complete. Her story was a very simple one. She had been living country fashion with her murderer for nearly a year. During the few months previous to the assault the other man had persistently thrust himself upon her, until at last her husband had warned her that he would kill her if he caught them together. On the day she was stabbed she had not even seen her would-be paramour enter the house, as she was working at the back, and seeing her husband approaching she went inside, and, to her astonishment, found the other man. She told him her husband was coming, and he ran away, and the former then entered and stabbed her, and she knew no more.

The exertion of the oath, and telling her innocent story, told sadly on her strength, and as the police already possessed the names of the two men, I told the nurse that no more was necessary beyond the names of any witnesses—but she could give none. The evidence was re-translated to "Tidankie," and in the presence of two witnesses she signed her first and last X, a sign symbolical of nothing to her, but having its origin in one of the most sacred epochs of the Christian faith.

Her deposition was only concluded in time, for after a few rambling incoherent sentences, which the nurse said were statements of her innocence, poor Tidankie, after a slight struggle and a faint rattling sound, passed away—an innocent victim, of childish age, of that jealous fiend which tortures all alike. Her murderer was never caught, and probably joined some interior tribe, knowing too well the fate in store for him if he were found in the colony.

On the way back to the office I passed a wedding-party going gaily to the Cathedral—the black bride, dressed in muslin and gauze, and the orange blossoms, without which even an African wedding would not be complete. She was sitting, proudly triumphant, in a bath chair, followed by many others with gaily-dressed occupants—the envy of the admiring crowd who trooped behind, laughing and shouting in high glee. While the men, in incongruously cut frock coats, bell-shaped trousers, and tall hats of antiquated build, smirked along, equalling, in conceit and pride of dress, the women they were accompanying. A drum-and-fife band was in attendance prepared to play them home vigorously and keep up an incessant rub-a-dub-dub until the following morning, by which time the happy couple would have expended several years' savings in entertaining their friends, and paying for the tawdry garments and finery.

The Timaneh oath, above written, is not the only peculiar form of oath known in the colony, for the Mendis adopt a somewhat similar one; and though their dialect is quite distinct, as are also their features and characteristics, this similarity may go to prove that they were once of the same tribe. The Mendis also use the two irons and speak as follows, but the guttural joining of "ng," or "nb," or "gb," are difficult to transcribe into pronounceable English: the "g" is, in these cases, always hard, the letter "j" would be used to show the "g" soft of orthoepy.

  O Ngawoh! yaie nge be leh fae,
  Nge—a giebe, wah sarie fah, tah be mori,
  Be ndei corrae, be le ndorgborhoo,
  Carrie e bench, be jeah dendehoo,
  Dendeh e lumboo, be lo njeyhoo be har,
  Be to torg-pornah, be gurrah ndormah be har;
  Garaie gpandeh gurrah bema be har,
  Keh, be tonyah, yeah lai, fong fainge!

Oh God! come down; thou giv'st me fowl.
(In) This case, I come as a witness, and I will speak.
If I tell lies, I go in the bush and serpent bite me;
If I go in a canoe, the canoe will sink and I drown,
If I climb a palm tree, I must fall and die.
You (God) let thunder fall and kill me.
If I talk the truth then I am safe in thee!

The oaths in each case show the knowledge of a higher spirit. To the Timaneh, he is "Pahtol," to the Mendi, "Wgawoh." In both cases, the penalties for giving false evidence, are invoked to injure them on earth. There is no trace of any belief in an existence hereafter, and in this we may find the key-note of many of their superstitions. What to them more natural than the invitation that the food entering a false mouth should be a curse? What stronger invocation to these people living in the bush teeming with snakes, or the river with crocodiles, that false evidence should bring them violent death? Or that, in climbing the high palm trees, or in using their canoes, they should pay the penalty of lying with their lives?

It will be observed that the dreadful alligator is only spoken of in the Timaneh oath, and this in a measure shows the difference that has grown up insensibly between these now distinct tribes. The Mendis are a nation living in larger towns on the seaboard, and in the interior.

With them, therefore, the snake appears to be a more common death than that of the alligator. But the Timanehs are a people divided into thousands of little villages living up narrow dank creeks, with their mud huts almost at the water's edge. Hence the alligator enters largely into the fears of their existence, and the oaths thus give slight testimony of these different characteristics.

The Mohametan oath on the Koran is probably well known, but the Kroo tribe also have a separate and distinct oath. The witness receives a small quantity of salt in the palm of his right hand; the person administering the same takes the hand and proceeds as follows in jerky sentences:

> " You nar muahbeh,
> We nu nahmarru,
> Plah Nyesuah!
> Wye bor seh poneh;
> You ne beh-cheh nah much."

> " This salt that you are going to take,
> The words you are going to talk,
> (Are in the) fear (of) God!
> If you talk lies,
> This salt will cut your belly."

The salt is then swallowed by the witness. These Kroo people are a peculiar race, and occupy a strip of country below Liberia. They are the sailors of the West Coast of Africa, as the "Seedie" boys are on the East Coast. Every man-of-war and mail steamer takes a batch of these men, who do all the hard work of the ship while on this deadly station. On board, they elect their own head-man, whom they will allow to flog them and drive them at their work as much as he pleases. In the navy, they are rated as seamen, and paid accordingly, receiving their discharge in the ordinary way when the ship leaves the station. But on merchant vessels they take a certain portion of their wages in gunpowder, spirits, and salt pork. As a race they are to be distinguished by a broad black band tattooed down their forehead, which shows up distinctly, notwithstanding their very dark skin.

There is a large settlement of them at Sierra Leone, and they all live in one part of the town known as Krootown. Here they have a local king, named King Tom, who is also a sergeant of police; and considering the sums of money they bring on shore when discharged they are quiet and easily managed. On the shore they are useless, and I doubt if one has ever been persuaded to leave the sea for any shore pursuit. Most of them have at one time or other served on board a British war vessel, and they invariably retain the names under which they were entered in the ship's books on their first voyage. Hence, among them we have John Bull, Union Jack, Two Glass, Bull's-eye, Deadlight, Billy Starboard, Rope Yarn, Ned Hatchway, Pea Soup, Plum Duff, and a host of other names which they are very proud of.

As with the Timanehs and Mendis their oath also acknowledges the existence of a Divine Being called " Nyesuah," whilst its form shows their habits and existence. For their lives are associated with salt from their earliest infancy to their grave.

There are numerous other divisions of the African race having representatives in the colony, the Soo-soos, a warlike and savage tribe occupying territory adjacent to Sherboro, whose swords are ever ready to be used in return for plunder and slaves; the Ebos, perhaps the most peaceable of Africans, coming from the far interior, a good-natured hard-working race, but one generally put upon by the Akus, who are the Jews of Africa, with all the features and characteristics in the black race, which mark them out in the civilized world, having no fixed headquarters, but pushing themselves steadily forward in advancement through their shrewdness and cunning. The Loubahs or Loubies, a poor class of natives, of low order, living in the low-lying districts of the interior, in semi-starvation and idleness. While the Mandingos stand out in their Mohamedan glory, a distinct and compact race, wealthy in cattle and goods, building rude temples in the interior, and making their own weapons and clothes, but sticking steadfastly to their faith and their Arab traditions and habits of slavery.

CHAPTER XVII.

AN UNFORTUNATE HISTORY.

A YOUNG German named Henry von Alten[*] was brought to Freetown by a native, in a nude condition, having apparently suffered severely from the effects of exposure and hunger. His tale was a sad one, and created a sensation among us, while it became still more tragic by subsequent events.

Von Alten's parents were well-to-do people in Germany, and he had served through the Franco-Prussian war with distinction. Shortly afterwards, some youthful indiscretion, made it judicious that he should leave his home until the matter was arranged. His evil destiny led him to the West Coast, where he obtained a situation in a factory owned by a foreigner, situated up one of the northern rivers, but quite outside British jurisdiction.

---

[*] The name in this case is a fictitious one.

Judging by his employer's name, it would be concluded that he was of the same nationality as Von Alten; however, they soon disagreed, and the quarrel became so furious that his employer, with the assistance of his men, bound Von Alten hand and foot, and then not only flogged him, but made the natives do likewise. After treating the poor fellow in this way for two days, they drove him away from the factory, even refusing him any food, and made a bonfire of his belongings before his eyes.

Von Alten wandered about for several days in a starving condition, living upon such roots and herbs as he could gather, drinking the water from stagnant pools, and sleeping as best he could in the damp and dangerous bush. Fortunately, his wanderings led him to a small village on the borders of British jurisdiction. The poor natives behaved like good Samaritans, and gave him such food as they possessed. One of them then guided him through the bush to the Bullom shore, and, borrowing a canoe, brought him to Freetown. He was found to be in a high state of fever, and immediately admitted to the hospital, and with kind attention, gradually regained strength.

But it soon became evident that the indignities he had suffered had seriously affected his mind, and he rambled on incoherently, describing in heartrending terms how they had not only flogged him while tied up and helpless, but had committed other indignities as well. Strange to say, his insanity took the form that all his ill-treatment had been the result of a conspiracy to prevent his returning to Germany, and it soon became apparent that he had this idea with regard to his present detention in the hospital. He seemed incapable of grasping the fact that he was among friends, who would assist him, if necessary, in going home.

With this one exception, the poor fellow was sane, and he became much attached to our colonial surgeon, who took considerable professional interest in his case. But these rational interludes were always followed by violent reactionary attacks, and it became necessary to place Von Alten under the charge of keepers. This he much resented, considering that they were there to prevent his returning to his native land.

Late one evening he deceived his attendants by simulating sleep, and suddenly springing upon them, dashed them right and left, and made his escape from the hospital. Search was made for him for several hours without result, and it was feared that he had drowned himself. In the morning the head Krooman of the colonial yacht "Princess of Wales" reported that a white man was sitting on a large boulder of rock across the small bay known as King Tom's Bay.

As there were no houses in the vicinity, and through the telescope the man appeared to be hatless and scantily covered, the officer in command of the colonial yacht had the good sense to go in a boat and see what he was doing. It was Von Alten, but in a terrible condition. One arm had been torn away from the socket at the elbow joint. All the fingers of the other hand were gone, and there were serious wounds about the legs and body, the ribs in one place being quite bare. The poor fellow had evidently tried to swim across the bay, and had been attacked by a shark. Considering his wounds, it seemed wonderful that he should have survived through the night.

He was taken back to the hospital in an almost hopeless condition. In addition to the severe shock to his nervous system and the attack of fever that all injuries produce in Africa, it was necessary to amputate the arm, or rather the remnant of it, at the shoulder. Fortunately, in tearing the arm away, the shark had strangulated the arteries, otherwise Alten would certainly have bled to death. Skilful attention and a healthy constitution stood him in good stead, and he once more gradually recovered strength.

During convalescence there were less signs of insanity, and our surgeon began to hope that the last unhappy adventure might bring back his reason.

Von Alten's description of his escape was as follows: He could see that he was imprisoned, with the object of preventing him returning to Germany, and he therefore determined to escape on the first opportunity. He kept quiet, so as to throw the guards off the alert, and, observing that the hospital gate was open, he knocked down both of the attendants, and turning the corner outside the walls, ran down the steep descent of loose rubble into the sea. Knowing that search would be made for him, he waded up to his neck in the water, and hid in the shadow cast by a slaughterhouse, which overhung the water so as to carry away the offal and blood.

A boat, in its search after him, came so close that he was obliged to sink below the surface, in order to avoid recapture. After all was quiet, he swam boldly out into deep water, hoping to find an empty boat, in which it was his intention to proceed to sea, where he might be picked up by a passing steamer, and thus gradually work his way back to his native land.

After swimming for a little while, he felt something rush through the water and seize him by the body, and his heart misgave him as he thought he had after all been recaptured. He struck at the object, but to his horror found that he was battling for life with a shark. The brute suddenly seized hold of one of his arms, and after a short struggle, he felt a spasm of pain, and found that it was half torn away. Von Alten then described how he began to give up all hope, but wrestled on bravely with his savage foe, fighting for life as he had never fought before. Growing fainter and fainter, such weak resistance as he was able to offer was becoming feebler as the shark tore bit after bit of his aching body away, until suddenly, to his surprise, his feet touched the bottom. This gave him renewed hope; so, struggling desperately, kicking and using his lacerated limbs against the brute, he gradually forced himself backwards into shoal water, where the shark could no longer follow him. He then waded on shore, and sat on a rock near at hand, watching his late adversary as it swam to and fro disappointed of its prey. Here he sat through the still night— until the stars gradually waned—until the morning gun told him it was five o'clock, though it was still dark,—until the grey light of the early morning rapidly dawned, and the sun rose with his powerful blinding glare over the land,—until suddenly, in a dazed way, he was sensible of being lifted gently and placed in the bottom of an open boat, when kind oblivion came to the relief of exhausted nature, and all was blank.

Long before convalescence it became apparent that with returning strength Von Alten's set idea that he was a prisoner reasserted itself, and he had to be watched incessantly. But there is no cunning equal to that given by insanity, and the negro keepers, despite all cautions, were careless, so that once more the patient disappeared, and no one knew how or whither.

The closest search revealed no trace, no one had seen him escape, and it was feared that he had again rushed into the sea, with fatal results. After several days the colonial surgeon received information that a one-armed white man had been seen in the bush, towards the Sugar-loaf Mountains, which rose at the back of the peninsula, and cautious search led to Von Alten's recapture in a sad condition. During this time he had lived upon roots and wild fruits, while his madness, being unrestrained, had developed itself into a fixed mania.

Immediate arrangements were made for sending him home, and, carefully guarded, Von Alten reached Liverpool in safety, and there he once again escaped. After a few days he was accidentally discovered by a policeman, in a starved condition, hiding in some half-built houses on the outskirts of the town. The poor fellow was never destined to reach his country and home, for on the voyage from Liverpool to Hamburg he was found missing one morning, and it was surmised that he had jumped overboard during the night, probably with the one sad idea of returning to his native land : drowned, after all his adventures and vicissitudes, within sight of the Fatherland to which he yearned to return. And let it be hoped that kind fate cast his body on those shores to be buried among those friends whom he had died in striving to reach. His ill-treatment had been inflicted outside British jurisdiction, and as both Von Alten and his employer were foreigners, nothing was done to the man whose behaviour had resulted in the insanity and death of this poor fellow.

But many changes had taken place in the colony since my arrival. Many had gone away never to return, others were resting in God's Acre, humanely situated out of sight of the town where one could not see the never-ending processions. Our genial acting Governor suffered from recurring attacks of fever, which completely prostrated him, and it soon became apparent that he must lie invalided. Every day that he continued at his post was at the risk of life, and at last he was sent home. His place was taken by the Crown Solicitor, who, through being appointed acting chief justice, became administrator, under virtue of the royal warrant then existing for the government of the colony during the temporary absence of the governor.

Unfortunately, there is no such thing as

acclimatization on the coast. A man may have the good luck to live for many years without any fever at all, but suddenly one morning he will be missing, and the dreaded fever will have done its sharp work ere it was even known that he was ill. On the other hand, it is not uncommon for men to die of it within a few days of their landing, who have never been in the tropics before. There is no rule, and no safeguard against its insidious power: the teetotaler, or temperate man, will be carried off while the drunkard remains, the strong man of powerful physique will pass away like a child from an apparently slight attack, while an attenuated sickly individual will wrestle for weeks in delirious agony, and then slowly recover. The death rate undoubtedly increases with the increase of the white population. One only lives on the coast to be perpetually reminded of death in its awful suddenness, and " Vive memor lethi " should be every white man's motto sojourning in this unhealthy place.

But sickness and fevers are not the only discomforts of West African existence; for, during my residence the settlement was suddenly invaded with a plague of "chigos," or "jiggers," as they are corruptly called. These tiny insects, not unlike a minute flea, burrow into the skin, generally under the toe or finger nails. At first their presence is unknown, and then a slight itching sensation may be felt; but in a land of prickly heat and eczema this may pass unnoticed. Then a slightly discoloured swelling appears, which may be felt occasionally tender, and you will then know that about ten thousand "jigger" eggs have been deposited in your body. The insect is then in a sack about the size of a small pea; and it is advisable to remove this sack, with its thousands of unhatched eggs entire. The natives are very deft at removing these, and they carefully cut all round the flesh, which will be sore and require tender treatment for many days, as abscesses have resulted from their neglect. The "jigger" sack contains the female in the centre, and her eggs all round, and it is advisable to burn them, as neither water or smashing seems to be fatal to their hatching powers. To disregard one of these deposits would be most serious, as after the eggs are once hatched the insects spread rapidly over the body, and it would be almost impossible, without amputation, to save first the toes, then the leg, and even life. Among the natives on the Coast, especially the Kroomen below Liberia, "jiggers" have been most disastrous, and the disgusting appearance of a man's leg half eaten with "jiggers" can be more easily imagined than described.

Hitherto these pests had been absent from Sierra Leone, but whether they came up by some ill wind or not it was impossible to tell, "Jiggers" were almost the only talk, and the usually harmless expression of "You be jiggered!" was felt to be an unkind wish. The thickest boots were useless in repelling them. They invaded the streets and the houses, upstairs and downstairs alike, and the only safeguard was to make your boy "jigger"-hunt over your body several times during the day. The ignorant natives at last organised open-air ju-ju meetings for relief from further "jiggers;" and having excited themselves into a fanatical fury, they chased the imaginary "jiggers" into the sea, beating the ground as they ran along. After a while the "jigger" was accepted as a necessary evil, and we tried to congratulate ourselves that it was nothing worse. So far, at all events, the Guinea-worm had not visited the settlement, and one had not to reel off so many yards of worm every morning before breakfast.

But fortune was not kind, for as soon as we became as reconciled as circumstances would permit to the "jiggers," one of the army surgeons discovered that the beef of the colony was quite unfit for food, being infected with "cyster circe cellulosæ," or the larvæ of tapeworms. To all outward appearances the cattle were fat and healthy, but when slaughtered, the meat was found to be pregnant with these loathsome and dangerous germs. Day after day whole carcasses were seized by the sanitary inspector, and one's magisterial duties were increased by their being brought to the doors for the necessary order for their destruction as unfit for human food, which could only be given upon inspection of the meat. It was most unpleasant and disagreeable work, and I would prefer at any time to cross a street rather than pass a butcher's shop with its hanging carcasses of lately killed animals.

The unfortunate army contractor suffered severely, for he was compelled to tender so much beef per diem for the use of the troops, and when it was condemned he had to buy substitutes at very heavy prices. Other provisions became much dearer in consequence, and our food supply limited to fish and fowl, and occasionally a little mutton. These germs possessed such vitality that no ordinary amount of cooking would kill them, and even had that been possible, beef is one thing and tape-worm larvæ another. In about a year the disease gradually died away, though the animals continued to feed on the same pasturage, and we gladly returned to the somewhat tough beef of the colony.

CHAPTER XVIII.

A "LEOPARD" ADVENTURE.

THE refreshing Harmatan (pronounced har-ma-tan') breeze which preceded another rainy season was blowing steadily, so the "Wave" was in great request as she went skimming over the surface of the broad estuary. As I had not been on a trip for some months, I applied for a few days' leave of absence, which were readily granted. A young fellow in the Army Medical Department who had recently arrived at the settlement agreed to accompany me, and we carefully stocked the larder with provisions for ourselves and men, while a few presents for the headmen of the villages we were going to visit were not omitted.

Leaving the boathouse at 3 a.m., we rowed across the river to Tagreen Point, where we arrived shortly before daybreak. By starting thus early in the morning we were able to make the most of our time, and also get two hours' shooting among the bush fowl and pigeons, which are fairly plentiful in the cassada plantations growing round Fenkleh. The Timaneh inhabitants of the little town, built, as is always the case in Timaneh towns, close to a huge silk cotton tree, were considerably surprised to see the " Wave " at anchor at such an early hour in the picturesque bay, and they followed our procession up the principal street to the enclosure of the headman, from whom I desired to obtain a house in which we could rest throughout the heat of the day.

All African towns are very much alike, and a description of one answers for nearly all, the exception being that, in the interior, strong stockades are built round them for safety. The houses are round, and made of mud ; the roofs are conical and made of thatch ; the floors are made of dung and earth well beaten until it forms a cement. In the larger ones, a raised step is made of the same material, and this answers for the bed, and the habitation is complete. Occasionally small lean-to's are added, but, as a rule, if the house is not large enough an additional one is built inside the compound. The yards belonging to the houses are circular, and around these the other houses for the remainder of the family are built, the entrances all facing inwards. A bamboo or wattle fence connects the outer ring between the walls of the houses where they do not touch. Each family thus has its own enclosure and maintains its privacy. In another part of the town there will be a palaver house—a roofed covering raised on open piles. This is the exchange, or bazaar, where all public matters are discussed, and here of a moonlight night they meet to gossip and smoke. On idle days, others may be seen in it squatting on the ground playing the African game of "worrah," a kind of backgammon, played with beans, on a board rudely made in the shape of a canoe, with small pockets or divisions, into which the players put their pieces. As there is no distinctive mark between the counters of either side, it is difficult to understand in what the game consists. But the natives are very fond of it, and it appears to require as much profound study as chess, for they become deeply absorbed in its intricacies, while they are able to leave it off and resume it at another time without apparent loss of interest in its result.

The headman soon placed an inclosed pavilion at our disposal, and we started out with our guns. Owing to the gradual increase of the heat, the morning is not such a pleasant time for shooting in the tropics as late in the afternoon. The sun increases in power so rapidly that by eight o'clock it is too hot for enjoyment, and the birds grow scarcer. However, we knocked over several brace of bush fowl, and many more pigeons, which are, I think, the better eating of the two. Our only misfortune was getting into a leech swamp, and the howls of our bare-legged boy following with the game-bag, amused us greatly, until we found ourselves hopping about, slapping our legs and thighs, with the disadvantage that our smalls prevented us getting rid of these troublesome pests.

How different the mud hut looked when we returned. Two camp beds with mosquito curtains graced the sides, a small table with tempting fruit on it was neatly laid, while the delicious smell of newly-roasted coffee whetted our already sharp appetites. Despite numerous touches of fever and failing health, one could not but enjoy such a holiday. We fed, and then lay down and smoked until the heat of the day passed away. We had had enough of Fenkleh, however, so, rewarding the headman and the owner of the hovel, we resumed our journey.

The afternoon breeze carried us smoothly along up the river, here perfectly navigable to large vessels, past numerous islands all fringed with the mangrove bush whose roots intertwined in fantastic shapes, while the overhanging leaves drooped gracefully in the running water. Although the river is studded with islands, very few of them are inhabited or cultivated, though they vary in extent from three to a hundred acres, and more suitable land for rice cultivation could hardly be found.

All of these islands appear to be called " Tasso." " What island's that ? " I inquired. " N'a Tasso, massa." " And that one there ? " " Dat one, sah, n'a Big Tasso." " Yes, but this one here ? " " Dis one called Lilly Tasso, sah." " Well, but this one to the right, hasn't that also a name ? " " Yes, massa, dat n'a Tasso too." Nor could I ascertain that the Government had any distinguishing names for them. The one to which we were bound as our next halting-place had two villages in it : the town along the river beach peopled by Sierra Leonians, and a native town nearly on the opposite side occupied by Mandingos.

After a pleasant sail of two hours, during which we were lucky enough to shoot a white-headed fish eagle, we ran the boat on the sandy beach, where a lot of natives had gathered to receive us on landing.

An African in apparently well-to-do circumstances, for he wore boots, came forward and offered his assistance, which we gladly accepted. He soon obtained a house, and it was quite a luxurious dwelling, though only built of mud. The walls were neatly whitewashed and picked out in colours, while various coloured prints. including a portrait of our Queen, were hung round the room. The house belonged to a Mrs, Johnson, a trader on the rivers, and she was fat, forty, and very good-natured, thinking nothing of the inconvenience of turning out for our benefit. Hearing that there was some sport to be had close by, the man procured me a guide, who led me to the bed of a dry lake covered with thick grass, and quite six acres in extent. Towards the end of the rains my guide informed me that it was full of water, and many aquatic birds might then be shot. But in its present dry state it was a pretty sight, a bright green bed of springy turf, a perfect oval in shape, fringed round at regular intervals with tall trees whose leaves of varied tints shone in the sun, now slowly descending in the far West; while a thick fringe of bush grew round the edge, marking the line to which the water rose in the rainy season. The place was alive with wood pigeons and doves, and there were also many of the beautiful green pigeon with bright scarlet beak, no specimen of which has as yet ever been known to live in captivity.

In the evening we strolled over to the Mandingo village, having sent forward notice of our approach. A few bottles of rum and some showy handkerchiefs paved the way to good feelings, and at our desire a native dance was arranged. The musicans and dancers sat in a circle, those who were not dancing clapping their hands in time with the music, while the dancers in the ring worked themselves into a state of excitement by the energy of their gyrations; quicker played the peculiar shaped instruments; faster went arms and feet, the more excited they grew, while a sort of major domo walked round and encouraged them to increase their violent exertions.

In the early morning we prepared to continue our voyage, and thanked our hospitable landlady, who declined accepting any payment for the use of her very comfortable and clean little house. But just before embarking, our male friend of the previous day came up and handed me what he called his little account, which I think deserves to be published.

	£	s.	d.
To searching and procuring a house, and rent for the same, per one night.	1	1	0
To finding one boy (the man's son) to act as guide on shooting expedition, and wages for the same	0	4	6
To acting as interpreter at Mandingo Town ...	0	5	0
To extras for accommodation for men, etc., including candles	0	15	0
E. & O. E.	£2	5	6

"Are you quite sure that you have omitted nothing?" I asked sarcastically.

" He didn't think so, but would be very glad if the gentleman would give him a little present for himself."

I then congratulated him upon the manner in which he had made up his account, when he informed me that he had been a lawyer's clerk in

Freetown, and the bill would certainly bear testimony to that assertion.

I next informed him that Mrs. Johnson had refused to take any rent, and as I had paid the boy for guiding me to the lake, it was only necessary to deal with his own valuable services.

He said, in these circumstances he would take a guinea in satisfaction of his claim, and give a receipt for the full amount. But this did not satisfy me, so I offered him a halfcrown, which he indignantly refused, until seeing that we would be off in a few minutes without his getting anything, he accepted it, and begged very hard for a bottle of rum to be thrown in, when he went away quite contented.

From Tasso Island the river still continues in a broad and deep channel as far as Rotomboh, a small settlement on the right bank, on a jutting promontory. Close by, on a headland, is a factory belonging to Messrs. Verminek, built in the Swiss chalet style. This stands out picturesquely on the broad and open river, midst scenery devoid of natural cultivation, the only other habitation visible being some miles further up, where we had arranged to break our journey until the heat of the day had passed. At this small town we were most courteously received by the headman, who, without hesitation, placed his house at our disposal, while his wife insisted upon personally looking after the breakfast, for which the pull in the face of the harmatan had fully prepared us.

In conversation with him I elicited the information that big game was frequently seen near the village, and he sent for a man who was positive that if we would consent to stay out in the bush all night, and bait the place with a kid, we should probably succeed in finding a tiger (leopard). We readily agreed to remain under such circumstances; and oblivious of the heat, I went with the guide to inspect the spot. He led me for about an hour by bush paths through the dense jungle to a ravine, down which a burn was gently running, and from what I had read in books, I imagined this would be just the place likely to be frequented by leopards.

The plans were soon made : we, that is Callaghan and myself, would climb two neighbouring trees, and tether the young goat to a stump about fifteen yards off in the direction of the running water. On my return, Callaghan was as keen as myself at the prospect of such big game, and when the sun had gone down, we set off, with a couple of rugs to make our perches more comfortable; while the guide led a wretched kid by a string. Arrived at the spot, the doomed kid was tethered by a leg to the stake, and we climbed into our respective positions, to await events.

Until darkness completely set in we were jolly enough, and after that for some time we continued talking and smoking, when it was decided that watchful silence must be observed. After what appeared an interminable period, I could stand it no longer, and the wretched kid was bleating incessantly; so I shouted, "How are you—comfortable?" "Comfortable indade! I'm sore all over, and have a crick in me back," answered Callaghan ruefully. "What's the time?' he added.

"Only a quarter to nine!" I replied with a groan.

"Faix, I can't stand this until morning. Shure, if these are the pleasures of huntin', I'll retire after it. I've strapped meself to the tree like a martyr to the stake," said Callaghan.

"I am tied up, too," I answered. "But you try and sleep for two hours, and I will keep watch, and then it will be your turn, as it will never do to continue talking."

"Right you are, me boy; so, good night."

"Good night," I replied; and relighting my pipe, I tried to make music out of the repeated bah-ings of the wretched kid, which was performing its task to perfection. The stillness, only broken by the incessant humming of the insects, the regular croaking of the frogs, and the steady cries of the kid, had a most sleepy effect upon me, while the trees cast fantastic shadows over the ground. Notwithstanding the discomfort of my position, my head kept drowsily falling forward. Callaghan, as far as I could judge, had utterly collapsed, and at last I also forgot my vigil, and dropped asleep.

"Whist," said Callaghan.

"I'm awake," I answered, with a guilty start.

"Arrah, hould your tongue. I heard something rustling, and the kid's making an uncommon noise."

I made no answer, but the expressive clicking of four hammers was distinctly heard.

"The leopard!" I cried excitedly in a low voice, as a dark shadow sprang across the narrow space.

"Shure, it's ateing it already," answered Callaghan. "Let us fire together when I count three. One—two—three."

Bang—bang!—and all was still.

"Be ready with the other barrel if it moves. It's no use spoiling the skin by riddling it unnecessarily," I said.

"Faix, it's as dead as a nail," said Callaghan.

"So I think, too, but get down and see," I answered.

"Divil a fear of me. I've always read that leopards are mighty dangerous in their death struggles. Shure, it's not such bad fun, afther all. Won't the boys up at the mess be surprised?" cried Callaghan, elated.

"How it sprang upon the kid," I said.

"It did, indeed," was the rejoinder. "What's the time?"

"Nearly four, I am glad to say."

So we emptied our flasks in good spirits, and tried to forget the discomforts of our long vigil. However, there's an ending to everything, and at the earliest glimpse of dawn we descended, and with carefully loaded guns, approached the spot. Callaghan was slightly ahead, and as he parted the long grass, he tilted his cap forward

"SHURE! IT'S TWO GOATS WE'VE SHOT, AND NOT A LEOPARD

in a peculiar way affected by Irishmen, as he scratched the back of his head.

"Is it quite dead?" I asked.

"Ay, the pair of them; and a divil of a mess we've made of it. Shure, it's two goats we have shot, and not a leopard at all." And there before us lay the nanny and her kid, the love of the mother having brought about the doom of both, as instinct and the bleatings of the kid had enabled her to trace it to the fatal spot.

"What are we to do now?" I said.

"Well, I think we had better say nothing about it, and get on with our journey as fast as possible," suggested Callaghan.

"That will never do; it's sure to be found out. We had better pay up manfully, and brave it out," I answered. "I say, Callaghan, won't the boys up at the mess be surprised," I added, sarcastically.

"Now, look here. Shure, ye'll not go tellin' the boys up yonder (at the mess). It's leaving the place I'd have to be."

"Certainly not, old fellow; if you won't say anything down below (in the town),' I gladly responded. "Honour bright, you know?"

Callaghan: "Honour bright it is, and you'll never catch me moonlightin' again, I promise ye, for me back's broke, and me neck nearly dislocated, independent of our having slaughtered a poor goat and her kid."

CHAPTER XIX.

A LOKKOH PALAVER AND DANCE.

A FEW miles higher up, the river rapidly narrowed, and we were within a short distance of Lokkoh, an important native town situated on the highest navigable part of the Sierra Leone river. The creek leading to it is broader than that to Waterloo, and after passing half way up it, there is a complete change in the scenery on the banks. The low mangrove bush that had fringed the sides lower down was replaced by high mossy banks, with tall and tangled ferns upon which numerous tropical plants cluster in wild confusion. The gorgeous red hybiscus, and the lovely arum lily of waxen hue, with its beautiful deep-green leaves, being entangled round the trunks of the twisted frangipani, and wild casti with long strange blossoms, and orchids sprouted from huge fungoid bulbs on the thick branches of the heavy trees. The stately palm, with its lofty smooth stem, topped by many feet of brilliant green bark, swelling out in rounded symmetry, over which its foliage dropped in graceful pleasing curves, swaying up and down with gentle sound in the light breeze.

Within a few yards of the landing-place we shot at an alligator on the banks, but he plunged into the stream with a loud splash, while the noise of the guns brought the natives rapidly down to the muddy landing-place. Notwithstanding that this is an important African town, and one through which much trade passes overland to and from the interior, there is no wharf, in the civilized meaning of the word. The natives are content, as there fathers were before them, to wade, or be carried through the mud and slime to the shore or to the canoe. About fifty yards higher up, the creek terminates in a small waterfall, down which the water is now trickling, but in a few months the heavy rains will make it a swollen torrent; above this, the river becomes a shallow running stream over rocks and jutting stones.

In accordance with the usual custom, we

proceeded to the Alekarli's house, and waited in the palaver chamber until he came out. His house would be considered a palace in the interior, though only made of mud. It is a long rambling building, not built in the usual conical style, and boasts of small windows and doors, which are painted in bright colours, quite in keeping with the native love of contrast. The palaver chamber is about fifty feet long, and had a raised mud seat all round it, built into the walls, while at the upper end there is a small raised platform, also built of mud.

Chairs had been brought out for our accommodation, and the natives arrived in batches and sat round the room. There was to be a palaver, in consequence of our arrival, evidently, and I told Callaghan we must stick up for getting on the platform along with the chief and his principal followers. The Alekarli entered with several of his head-men, all intelligent-looking fellows, and as we exchanged friendly greetings, one of our men translated to him that we were pleased at having met him, as he is so often away at more important towns in the interior; and we quietly followed him on to the platform upon which our chairs were brought up.

The Alekarli then made a speech in Mandingo, in quiet tones, pausing while it was translated to us, and emphasising his remarks with easy self-possession. He was an old fellow, with long white beard and fine features, and his flowing gown of simple blue baft sat in graceful folds on his lithe figure. "Tell the two English that they are welcome to my country: one we know of as a Government Secretary, for who among you has not heard of his boat in which he sails about the rivers both by night and by day? A canoe from Freetown told me of their coming, and I am glad, for they come as friends by day, and we must not be backward in giving them welcome. To him and his friend we give a hearty welcome, for they are of the great nation with whom we are at friendship and peace, and whose wealth is our wealth, and we greet them among us."

To this I replied: "Tell the Alekarli how pleased we are to visit Lokkoh, and how very clean the town is. Tell him that this pleasure is much increased by meeting him: his kingdom is large, and we are glad to have shaken his hand. Tell him that he is always spoken of as a friend by us, and when men pass hands as friends, it means they are at one together, for the heart speaks from the hand of welcome. We would wish to stop the night in the town, if he would give us a house, for on the next day we must return, 'and peace be with him.'"

"Callaghan! you must say something," I said.

"All right, me boy, it's meself that has kissed the blarney stone. Tell the old gentleman that he's a thunderin' fine fellow with his handsome beard."

"Sah!" said the astonished interpreter.

"Tell the Alekarli," I said, "that this gentleman says he has heard he is a great chief."

Callaghan continued: "Ay, that's it. And tell him he's received us like a gentleman, and I'm proud to make his acquaintance."

"I beg your pardon, sah, I no quite sabbe," said the confused interpreter, turning to me.

"Oh, tell him that my friend says he has welcomed us as a true white man's friend, and that he wishes him well." (Loud cries of "Hi-hi," from the audience.)

"Tell him," added Callaghan, raising his voice, "if ever he comes to Freetown and cloimbs the hill to the officers' mess, not to forget to ask for Jim Callaghan; I think that will fetch him," he added, turning to me.

"Tell him," I said to the dumfoundered interpreter, "that when next big palaver takes place at Freetown, that we hope to see him as well as he is now, with plenty of his people to make big dance, and that we wish to pass hands before leaving in the morning."

Callaghan's remarks were much appreciated, and, as he raised his voice, thinking by talking loudly to make his meaning plainer, the evident embarrassments of the interpreter were perceptible to the audience, who indulged in frequent cries of approval as he spoke.

In the evening the usual dance took place. It was on a much grander scale, and the performers were better up to their work than those at Tasso Island. Two of them, a man and a woman, excelled all the others. If one of these entered the ring, the other soon followed, and the rest of the dancers dropped away. The man had on a white goat-skin cap, strips of the skin hanging to his shoulders, and a loin cloth, and as he whirled round and threw his head about, it gave him a weird appearance in the bright moonlight. The woman wore a short skirt

"SHE STOOD STILL, AND THE MAN ALMOST ENCIRCLED HER."
See p. 237.

to the knee, and fastened under her shoulders, leaving her arms bare, and she swung them about with an undulating motion, while she danced no less vigorously than the man.

It was apparent that these two were the principal characters in a rude plot. The man danced round the ring in wild movements, and the woman, forming an inner ring, did the same, gradually decreasing the circumference. When the woman arrived in the centre, she stood still, and the man almost encircled her, as he flew round and round, until he suddenly stopped as if to look at her. Then, by a quick movement, the woman completely altered her shape, bringing her back nearly on a level with her head, a horrible contortion, and the man then reversed the dance by rapidly increasing gyrations, until the outer edge was again reached. The other dancers then rushed in, as in a ballet at home, thus giving breathing time to the two principal performers. On the next occasion the man took the inner station, while the woman encircled outside until the centre was reached, where he stood still, while the woman kept spinning round him, and then also stopped and again raised her back. As she did this the man threw his body backward, as if to avoid her clutches, until the whole of his back was lying on the ground, while the legs up to the knee remained in a standing position. This was a wonderful acrobatic feat and devoid of the repugnance of that of the woman. The man's body appeared to form no circular curve: to the knee his legs were upright, from the knee to the back they slanted to the ground, and the rest of the body was flat upon it. He performed this trick several times and had no difficulty in raising himself again into an upright position.

The plot was simply a man making advances to a woman whom, to his horror, he finds deformed after his exertions to gain her, and his action in throwing himself back was a dumb expression of horror at the discovery of her deformity. We amply rewarded the players and musicians, and retired early after a somewhat fatiguing day, while our previous night's discomfort made us enjoy our comparatively luxurious beds.

Having said good-bye at an early hour to the friendly chief, we rowed down the creek and found the Harmatan blowing strongly, so, hoisting all sail, the "Wave" went along at a rattling pace, assisted by the ebbing tide. The origin of these Harmatan winds, apparently rising in the interior and bringing down clouds of dust, has never been scientifically explained. These differ entirely from the dust storms of Southern Africa, for they are not unpleasant, nor is the sand perceptible, except on the distant horizon, where it assumes the appearance of a heavy veil. On the body the wind has a most refreshing effect, and its dryness, caused by the minute particles of sand, braces up the constitution and makes the water refreshingly cold. An idea of the dryness of the atmosphere can be better imagined when it is stated that heavy furniture creaks and opens during a strong Harmatan, while lamps, jugs, and basins fly into pieces by the contraction. Sitting at a dinner party on one occasion during the Harmatan, the table burst open with a heavy detonating sound, like the crack of a miniature cannon, and several of the glasses and plates were broken in pieces.

The "Wave" was soon abreast of one of the "Tasso" islands, upon which are the dismantled ruins of a slave stronghold. The island is now uninhabited, and the natives have a suspicious belief, not to be wondered at, that it is still haunted by evil spirits, while there is a legend that a large rock standing boldly out in midstream, is the devil's stepping stone to the shore, but was originally intended to have been dropped upon the island by a good spirit, and thus destroy the baracoon. We landed and inspected the ruins, and found that even the steep ascent to them had evidently been cut away in days gone by, as a safeguard against capture. Several dismantled cannon still lie about, while the thickness of the walls, their height, and large caverns, show that it must have been a place of great strength and considerable size. One or two pieces of rusty shackles, and small underground cells, still exist, to tell the tale, the nature of the trade that was carried on ; while the loopholed bastions, and general design of the fortifications, prove that the station was prepared to be defended against marauding enemies.

Rapid tropical vegetation is quickly moving these traces of a past history, and trees force their way through the crumbling ruins, bursting them asunder in a way which must be seen to be believed. A short distance from the fort are two gravestones, on one of which the word "sacred" could still be faintly traced. Beneath these lie the owners at one time or other of this once powerful stronghold, through which valuable cargoes of "black ivory" were once shipped to civilized ports: shipped to undergo the horrors of the middle passage, packed as even cattle dare not be packed at the present day, while a few miles lower down the river, but "a century after," there is a populous thriving town, composed entirely of a free people, among whom are probably some whose parents were once enchained within these crumbling walls.

But we were soon again scudding before the pleasant breeze, and arrived in good time at Freetown to find the outward-bound mail had come in, bringing its burthen of letters and papers from friends at home.

CHAPTER XX.

GENERAL EVENTS.

SIR SAMUEL ROWE was not to return amongst us, having been appointed by Her Majesty to the more lucrative government of the Gold Coast, and speculation was rife as to who was likely to be appointed to Sierra Leone; for it is a matter of extreme moment to a colonial official who is to be his superior.

Our mind was soon set at rest, since one of the Foreign Consuls received a dispatch from his government notifying that Mr. Arthur Havelock (now Sir Arthur Havelock) was to succeed Sir Samuel Rowe. As an instance of the interest taken by foreign governments in colonial matters, it was notable that the news was received in this way some weeks before the acting Governor was informed of the appointment by the Colonial Office.

Sir Samuel Rowe had done good work for the colony, having taken it over in a state of financial depression and disorder, and in a few years, by hard work and careful organisation, he established it on a satisfactory footing. His knowledge of the natives, especially of the interior, was very great, and he was feared and respected by them all, without ever proceeding to bloodshed, notwithstanding the many expeditions he undertook upon most delicate local affairs.* However, during his lengthy absence, matters had again become the reverse of orderly, and things were in such a state, that it would soon be proved whether or not his successor was equal to the trying ordeal of governing a colony with so many conflicting interests.

Governor Havelock, who was accompanied by Mrs. Havelock, at once proved himself to be made of sterling stuff, and idle heads of departments, who had been neglecting their own duties to interfere with those of other officers, soon had to change such undesirable habits. The Governor worked hard himself, and in a most

---

* By special request of the Liverpool merchants, Sir Samuel Rowe has since been reappointed to Sierra Leone with increased emoluments.

systematic manner, and he not only expected, but insisted on his officers doing the same. He was ever courteous, kindly, and firm, and, away from the office, his cheery manner and pleasant conversation won general approval. In a few months, under his rule, the Civil Service of the colony was more like such a service ought to be than I had ever seen before, and the work was carried on with perfect official regularity.

The long hours of 7 to 9 and 11 to 5, so disagreeable and hard upon the native officials, many of whom lived a long way from the office, and so trying to the English officials, were discarded for the regular hours of 10 to 4, upon the strict understanding that all arrears should be worked off in a given time. The effect was magical; the natives worked willingly and quickly, in order to show their appreciation of a kind action, which enabled them to have a few hours of daylight for their own purposes.

It was really laughable to witness the various attempts made by the officials to curry favour with the new Governor, by ascertaining his weak points (if indeed he ever showed any), so as to gain promotion at his hands. The church, hitherto neglected by almost all, received an increase in its congregation when it became evident that the Governor was a regular attendant. Those men who had become Catholics under a Catholic Governor, absentees under an absentee Governor, Dissenters under a Dissenting Governor, now became vigorous high churchmen under a High-Church Governor.

On the first Sunday, Governor and Mrs. Havelock turned to the east during the creed; on the following Sunday two officials and a boy did likewise. On the third Sunday about twenty of the congregation right or left-faced as the case might be, in order to take up the required position, whilst one or two others, in order to out-Herod Herod, seemed never to enter the church until after the Governor, and then made a marked and profound obeisance to the altar table on their way to their pews. The clergyman who was acting as colonial chaplain was desirous of gaining the vacancy. He had previously ignored all ceremonious observances, for he belonged to the C.M.S., but he now displayed an unaccountable inclination to turn his back on the congregation. After several Sundays he took a quarter turn to the east, and increased it Sunday by Sunday until he had gained the required position. But his heart misgave him, or an observant correspondent of the C.M.S. might object, so for some time his head turned towards the body of the church, while his body faced the head. Kind-hearted people said this was done that all should hear. Alas for this theory. It did not continue, and acoustic necessities were forgotten when choir boys were dressed in surplices and endeavoured vainly to chant the Psalms.

And the Governor. Was he pleased? If so, he showed no sign. None of the suddenly pious received one hair's breadth of favour or attention other than his official work entitled him to, and it soon became evident that the best way to please him as an official, was to do your duty to the best of your ability; and as a private citizen, to encourage law, order, and propriety, and leave him alone.

The form of Government of the colony underwent many changes after its acquisition by the Crown, and if the most beneficial arrangement has not at last been found, it has not been for want of trying different plans. But the early history of the colony has already been dealt with, and it is only necessary to mention those changes of recent years. In 1863 it was considered advisable that a change should be introduced, so as to enable the Governor for the time being to be assisted by two councils, one a legislative and the other an executive body. The latter consists of official members only, their proceedings being secret, and their duties to advise the Governor on any point upon which he desires to consult them, and their opinions are frequently transmitted to the Secretary of State for consideration, whether in support of, or against, any proposition. The Legislative Council is of a more public character, and contains a certain number of life members, nominated by the Governors and appointed by the Secretary of State. There is always a preponderance of official votes in the Legislative Council, and the Governor is entitled to enforce these votes in favour of any measure which he considers for the good government of the colony, though it may be an unpopular measure to the unofficial body.

In 1865, a new charter was issued bringing the whole of the possessions on the West African Coast, viz., the Gambia, Sierra Leone, the Gold Coast and Lagos, under one Government-in-Chief, to be called the West African

Settlement. Sierra Leone was to be the seat of Government, and retained its Executive Council, while separate Legislative Councils were established in each of the others to assist the lieutenant-governors with their advice. But this arrangement was found not to work well, the territory was too extended to keep touch, and the interests of each colony so entirely separated that in 1874 the Gold Coast and Lagos were made into a separate Government, since which they have again been divided. Sierra Leone and the Gambia still remained under one Governor-in-Chief, though another new charter had to be passed in 1874, which has been again revised in 1885.

In the Executive Council the most serious questions are considered, and although the Governor has power of life and death, these are never exercised without consultation with his Executive Council.

The life members of the Legislative Council are selected from well-to-do merchants and traders in the settlement, and at the present moment contains many natives who have raised themselves after years of hard work to such a position as to make their selection thoroughly deserved. Nothing can exceed the judiciousness of such a step. It is, in a measure, teaching the natives the power of self-government, while it proves that the question of colour is not considered as it was some few years back. Every endeavour should be made to give self-reliance to the natives, for it is to them the colony must look for prosperity, since its climate renders a large white population an impossibility.

Our native member, Mr. J. B. Pratt, who is now dead, exercised the greatest influence over a large section of the natives, and though his knowledge of English was very limited, his acquaintance with African customs and character made his presence in the Legislative Council of extreme utility to the Government. There is one anecdote with reference to him which deserves chronicling, and it created much amusement at the time. Very expensive harbour works were undertaken at Sierra Leone, which much improved the facilities for trade, though built at a heavy cost. It became necessary to raise an additional loan to complete them, and the Governor brought the matter before the Legislative Council, explaining, as he thought lucidly, the objects and manner of

s

raising the required sum, ending his speech by suggesting that it would therefore be advisable to obtain a sum of twenty thousand on debentures at £5. Turning to Mr. Pratt he inquired if he followed him. "Oh, yes, I sabbe, I sabbe," answered Mr. Pratt. "You want to obtain a loan of 20,000 benches at £5 to finish de harbour."

"Just so, Mr. Pratt, then you will support my motion."

"Certainly, Gubnor, certainly," and the motion was carried.

When the council had ended, Mr. Pratt left at the same time as the Colonial Secretary, and accosted him as follows :—

"I say, Massa Secetary, who de debbil gwin to sit on dem twenty tousand benches, and who gwin to lend them? I should say, better get one tousand first and buy um right out."

Occasionally large caravans come down from the interior, gradually swelling in numbers as they descend, until the settlement is inundated with chiefs and their numerous followers, bringing down with them ivory, gold, and produce of the soil. They are sometimes months in arriving, and while they are in the colony it becomes quite a gay place. The Governor holds a grand palaver on these occasions under the trees of the picturesque lawn of Government House. The natives arrive in separate batches accompanied by their musicians, playing quaintly shaped string and reed instruments, and singing their rather monotonous dirges. They are habited in the gala dress of their countries, and armed with their curiously shaped cutlasses or scimitars, and the Government inspector arranges them in order of precedence on the lawn, with their followers squatting on their hams behind and around. Opposite, in semi-circular form, are ranged the chairs for the Governor and his staff of officials, and behind the Governor's chair a Union Jack hangs listless in the still air. To the left the guard of honour of handsomely-dressed West India soldiers are ready with regimental colours flying, while the band is prepared to strike up our National Anthem when the Governor is marshalled to his place. Such a ceremonial is imposing and natural, and would form a fitting picture for a painter's brush, as the different characteristics of negro face, dress, and manner, add to the novelty of the scene. Here stands Mr. T. G. Lausen, the Government interpreter, in his incongruous uniform, a kind of bastard cavalry officer's undress. He is a man of invaluable use to the colony, and when his services are lost to the Government, for he is of goodly age, it will be almost impossible to replace him. Although he is king of Popo, a not inconsiderable kingdom, in his own right, he has elected to serve her Majesty's Government, and for years he has fulfilled his difficult duties to the satisfaction of the many different governors who have come and gone in his day. Among the natives, away even to the far interior, he is known and respected, and a letter from him will be the best passport for any traveller voyaging into this unknown land. He can speak almost every known African dialect, and is never at a loss for a word, either in them or in English; while his translations of native speeches receive an additional charm by their short sentences, their repetitions of native formulas, and their simplicity of quaint English diction.

The Governor having arrived, chief after chief will be introduced, and the kindly words of welcome translated. This form having been completed, he will translate the speeches of the natives, as they each in turn make their replies, for a palaver is an important part of African diplomacy. One native speech impressed me so at the time that I cannot refrain from giving it to the best of memory. The emissary had arrived from Futah Jallen, and had never before seen the sea, nor the men that go down in big ships, and his words were spoken quietly, and with Arab-like expression.

"I am now old in years, and my eyes see not well. Your Excellency who represents England's Queen have welcomed us as friends. Her name is known in the far interior as ever good and peaceful. Desiring neither our territory nor our wives, and interfering not with our customs. But wishing to trade with us in friendship and faith. Allah is the one Allah, and has made the world. He has put upon it many nations, but all are not alike, and Allah knows best. Some are white as the day, some are as black as night, and others are like the shadows of the moon. Some are strong, others are weak, and Allah has so ruled it. What groweth in our land is not in yours, and what you have we want. So friendship in this wise doth us good, and we profit. War does us harm, and neither side can gain—no, not even the victor. My king greets you through me, and to him when I return will I present the beautiful gown in your Queen's name, and he will be pleased. What my eyes have seen that will I also talk. Men in rows, whose guns speak quicker than words can tell; houses on the mighty sea, with more men in them than many towns, and these men can climb the tall poles to the sky. The big guns that roar as loud as thunder after a flash like that of lightning in the dark sky. All this I will say, and more. I will convey your wish for more trade to pass, so it should be with friends who have passed hands. Allah be with you and keep you."

This speech at the time impressed me so much that I can repeat the substance, and if it differs at all, it is in loss of impressiveness and quaintness of words which it would be impossible to convey on paper. The palavers are followed by refreshments. Native music sounds on the lawn, and they dance their dances in joy and gladness. Many things strike the fancy of these children of the interior. A huge tiger skin belonging to Governor Havelock quite astounded one native chief, who expressed a belief that it must be a very unhappy country for human beings where such monsters existed. A musical box created quite a surprise, while the bath-room, which has an innocent tap, such as may be seen in any hairdressers, capable of letting on either hot or cold water at will, was looked upon with stupefied awe, "for how can cold and hot exist in the one pipe?" asked the chief, as he shook his head at this grave wonder.

Then there is the silver lining to these visits, the presents, both in kind and money, given to each by the Government to foster friendship and goodwill until the return march begins. Then with tum-tumming and song they proceed by the broad road, rapidly narrowing into the bush path, over hill and dale, torrent and stream, breaking off one by one at different roads, into the far interior, there to relate the wonders they have seen, and account to their masters for their stewardships in their journey to the English Colony, and their interview with the Queen's representative.

CHAPTER XXI.

EXPEDITIONS IN SHERBRO AND BATTLE OF TALLIAH.

EARLY in 1883 Governor Havelock received instructions to annex a considerable tract of territory extending from British Sherbro to within a few miles of the Republic of Liberia. This step was deemed advisable in order to secure the control of the Sherbro district, in which the trade had been much affected by the continued lawlessness and squabbles going on among the natives, who, it was hoped, under British rule, would soon settle down to orderly government.

To the regret of the English merchants and residents, and against the advice of those best capable of judging of the wisdom of such a step, it was decided to withdraw the head-quarters of the West India regiments from Sierra Leone, and merely maintain a garrison of one company there in future, whose work would be mostly taken up in looking after the barracks. This reduction having been definitively settled, much surprise was created by the arrival of a smart officer of the Royal Engineers with instructions to make elaborate drawings for a new and costly set of barracks higher up in the hills, where the troops would be useless to protect the town in the event of a sudden *emeute*. Thus, on the one hand, the regiment was busy preparing to depart and sell off condemned stores; while, on the other, an officer, specially detailed for the purpose, was energetically engaged in measuring and collaborating details for a most costly set of buildings, capable of accommodating double the present garrison.

The time had come round when Governor Havelock was going on well-earned leave. He had worked hard for the good of the settlement, and shown such ability and tact, that it was very much doubted whether he would again return among us. Fortunately, so far he had stood the climate remarkably well, and Mrs. Havelock had also happily survived the still greater risks which women run by sojourning in this unhealthy settlement.

Within a few weeks of his departure, troubles unexpectedly arose in the Sherbro district. The natives, always given to fighting among themselves, carried their depredations into territory which was clearly within the boundaries of the colony, and the acting local commandant advised that strong measures should be taken to suppress such disorders. Mr. Pinkett, who was administering during the Governor's absence, and had previously acted as governor, took very strong views of this matter, and determined to administer a sharp lesson to the marauding chief and his war-boys. Accordingly, a small expeditionary force of police, with their rocket battery, started for the scene of the disturbances, Mr. Pinkett and the law adviser, Mr. Tarleton, accompanying the force.

Gpowe (pronounced Gupow) was by no means dismayed when he heard of their approach, for he had been very successful in his conflicts with the natives around, and also, perhaps, believed that a demonstration only was intended.

The little force disembarked from the boats at the small native town of Gbap, which they recaptured from the enemy almost without resistance, and the advance was ordered on

Whymah, Hahoon, and Sennehboh, three strongly stockaded towns all close together, which were full of Gpowe's warriors. Several friendly native chiefs and their followers joined in the expedition. The Sherbro district lies very low, and there is much swamp and morass throughout. Consequently the march inland, under the glare of the tropical sun, with tangled grass and thorn, was exceedingly trying through an enemy's country. But while it is possible to retire behind a stockade, African tactics are seldom to engage in the open, besides which, the friendly natives scouring around, effectually prevented any possibility of a flank surprise. Across the deep swamp the officers were carried picky-back by the bare-legged natives, who think nothing of wading through these mud troughs. But it was a labour of difficulty to carry Mr. Tarleton, a man of much weight, and he only got across rather a deeper swamp than usual by a plentiful besprinkling of mud upon the white clothes he had unwisely adopted as the most suitable uniform for such work. He grumbled greatly at his splashed condition, especially as his face had not escaped, and the small supply of water was too precious to be used for such a trifling matter in a campaign. His muddy condition was made most annoying to him, and amusing to the rest, through the politeness of the native who persisted in acquainting him of the fact. First of all, a policeman near to him on the march, said, "Sah, I beg your pardon." "Well, what is it?" "Nudding, sah, but you've got puttah-puttah mark on your face." "What's 'puttah-puttah'?" demanded Mr. Tarleton, gruffly. "Mud," answered Mr. Pinkett, laconically. "Yes, I know, my man; go on," grumbled Mr. Tarleton.

Presently a sergeant who had been hunting up stragglers came along. After making his report to the acting Governor, he turned to Mr. Tarleton, and, with a military salute, said, "Sah."

"Well, what do you want?"

"I beg pardon, sah, but you've got puttah-puttah mark on your face."

"Go on, and do your work, man, and don't bother me," was the irritable rejoinder.

In a short time a boatman sidled up, and, pulling his cap in nautical style, said, "Sah."

"What is it you want?" demanded Tarleton, with a fierce gleam in his eyes.

"Nudding, sah, only to tell you dat you've got puttah-puttah mark——"

"—— your puttah-puttah," shouted Tarleton. "Go away. The next man that puttah-puttah's me, I'll knock him down—by Heavens I will."

It was not long before the acting Commandant came up; he had been looking after the friendly natives, and having made a few remarks to Mr. Pinkett, he said "Hallo! Tarleton; all right so far?"

"Yes," said Tarleton, in surly tones, looking towards his inquirer.

"Oh! I say, you have got a black streak of mud on your face."

Tarleton's face, despite the streak, was a study, and, after spluttering several incoherent sentences, he gasped, "Look here, stop the expedition for Heaven's sake; let every one of the white fellows tell me I'm covered with mud, and every nigger puttah-puttah me until I'm sick, and then, perhaps, we can proceed quietly."

However, it was useless: a corporal presently came from the front with a message from the Inspector of Police, and having delivered it, he looked at Mr. Tarleton and then said, "Sah."

"Now, my man, be careful, because I'm in a

rage. Unless you're on business, go away—I'm in a rage."

"I beg pardon, sah; I only wish to tell you, sah, that you've got puttah-puttah——"

"D——n it, I can't stand this any longer. Clear out! go away!" literally shrieked Tarleton at the astonished policeman, as he raised a thick stick and threatened the "bobby," who precipitately retreated, while the rest of the officers burst into a roar of laughter, which only increased his exasperation.

But there was now more serious work in hand, far ahead, through the bush, the first stockade was visible, from which the natives opened a smart fusilade, and jeered and insulted the force with all kinds of native epithets. It was, however, short work; a few rounds from the rocket apparatus soon made a breach through the fence, and after one or two rushes the police were inside, and the enemy beat a rapid retreat by the rear, followed by the friendly natives, who pursued them some distance. The other two stockades fell in a similar manner, the casualties on the enemy's side being rather heavy, while among the police no fatalities whatever had occurred. The enemy retired by inaccessible by-paths upon Talliah, whither it was impossible to follow them upon land, so after burning the three stockades the return to the boats was ordered after a very fatiguing day. But the work having been begun had to be completed thoroughly, for from Talliah Gpowe breathed vengeance all around, and destroyed and burnt several towns within our protectorate. Mr. Pinkett therefore decided that it was essential that he should be driven from this, his last stronghold. Fortunately, the accounts of the early expeditions, and the troubles arising therefrom, got into the newspapers at home, and the authorities countermanded their orders about reducing the garrison, and the head-quarters of the 2nd West were directed to proceed thither at once. The garrison arrived opportunely, and Mr. Pinkett made rapid arrangements for the expedition to Talliah. Accordingly two companies of the 2nd West, and about two hundred of the constabulary, with their rocket battery and two howitzers, under the command of Major Talbot, left Sherbro in a flotilla of boats and proceeded up the Small Boom river; Mr. Pinkett also accompanying the expedition. The first night was passed at Matabah, a small town in

British territory, which had been pillaged and depopulated by Gpowe, who left nothing but the bare walls standing.

Next morning the advance was continued up the river, and the enemy's scouts continually appeared on the banks and fired at the boats, but made no effective attempts to dispute its passage. The first stockaded town reached was Kwatamahoo, and as the enemy declined to surrender, the banks were rapidly gained and the soldiers and police drove them inside the stockade. The rocket battery was brought into play, and did its work with terrible effect, for the second round fired the town, and in a few moments the thatched-roofed huts and the stockade were in a continuous blaze. The troops were unable to render any assistance to the enemy in their awful plight, so a forced march was ordered on Hahoo, the next stockaded town, which was completely taken by surprise, the enemy retiring after a trifling resistance. As Hahoo was strongly defended, and full of provisions, a halt was decided upon, and every precaution taken against surprise, while the boats were hurried up by the river as fast as possible.

The boats arrived in good time, and in the

early morning the river was crossed, and the forced march to Talliah begun, an officer and a small contingent being left to guard Hahoo as a base to fall back upon if necessary. By now the allies had become largely augmented owing to the previous successes of the expedition. These natives were divided, and posted on the flanks of the column, and a badge issued, to be worn by them, so as to distinguish them from the enemy. Two ambuscades had been prepared on the route, but the enemy, after firing at random, deserted them upon the approach of the force. This showed the wisdom of the precautionary measure of having posted the friendly natives on the flanks, as the dense bush afforded ample facilities for a surprise. After two hours' fatiguing march, Talliah was sighted, and the enemy were posted in the open to repel the advance; but they were soon driven to take refuge behind the triple stockade, which was thus described by the correspondent of the *Standard* newspaper :—

Gbow had cleared the bush for about eight hundred yards round the outer stockade, which was a very formidable one, and well deserved its reputation for strength. The fences of the outer stockade were twelve feet high, and planted at intervals of a few inches, the piles being of great thickness, and closely interlaced top and bottom with pliant ligneous shrubs, making for native warfare an almost irresistible *chevaux de frise*. There were two inner stockades, and Gbow had under his command about two thousand warriors.

The disposition for the attack was soon made under Major Talbot's command ; Captain Jackson, of the Royal Artillery, in colonial employ, was placed in charge of the howitzers and rocket battery. The constabulary, mostly composed of well-drilled time-expired soldiers, who had been brought up to a high state of discipline, under Inspector Revington, were led by him, while the West India troops formed the supports, and made flank attacks in support of the native allies, who bravely rushed up to the stockade, which they endeavoured to escalade.

Gpowe had not been idle. All the roofs of the houses had been removed, and were stacked some distance away in the open, so as to prevent the town being fired. According to native custom, a special fetish had been invoked to give victory to their side, and the medicine man's order was that two first born infant sons were to be massacred in cold blood so as to propitiate the war gre-gre. This barbarous act had been carried out, and the war-boys' courage had been kept up to fighting pitch by dances and promises of heavy plunder. In order to allow no flinching, one of the most trusty and bravest of his men had been tied to the rear gate, and furnished with musket and sword, with orders to shoot any who tried to escape. Again I must quote the correspondent of the *Standard*, for my description is but written from hearsay.

The order to advance was given, and, by a succession of rushes, our men were taken to within sixty yards of the stockade, and poured in a most telling fire. The allies on the flanks behaved with the utmost gallantry, clambering up the stockades, only to be repulsed by the fire and spear thrusts of the enemy. Three times they obtained a footing inside, to be ruthlessly driven back, maimed and wounded.

The scene was a vivid and picturesque one—an African stockade under a blazing sun, the gay uniform of the soldiers, intermingled with the red fezzes of the police, and the almost naked bodies of our allies, the flash and rattle of the rifle, and the fiery tails of the rockets as they work their sinuous way into the enemy's lines; the fierce war cries of our allies, as, with swords in their mouths, they again and again endeavour to escalade the fence. But no enemy with inferior weapons, and crowded into a small space, such as were Gbow's people, could stand against the shells that, with such precision, were falling in the midst, and at length a footing inside is gained, the fence is forced outwards in many places, and our allies pour in.

Meanwhile, inside the stockade Gbow's men

were fighting bravely, spurred on by that redoubtable warrior, but it was a forlorn struggle. To most of them the huge twenty-five pounder rockets, with their fierce, lurid light, flying zigzag from side to side, and then bursting into thousands of fragments, were a horrid revelation. The shells, too, exploding in the thick of the closely-packed horde, shedding carnage all round, were enough to dismay the stoutest heart, and the wretched fellows, in their new-born fright, endeavoured to protect themselves from these missiles by putting iron pots and pans on their heads, while they stubbornly fought on to the death. But, as the above correspondent continues :—

There is no occasion for any more fighting; the enemy are routed, flying for their lives, but the work of death still goes on. The fierce Kessus, inflamed with the passions for revenge, pursue the enemy from stockade to house, from house to open country. No quarter is given or expected, the wounded are murdered as they fall, and the horrible custom of mutilation follows.

Gbow narrowly escaped capture, and was hotly pursued, throwing away in his flight his silver snuff-box, his sword, and whip, and even his embroidered gown. . . . . The defence had been an obstinate one, and the engagement lasted over three hours. Inside the town the sight was ghastly in the extreme. In a small space one officer counted eighty-two dead; in another part twenty-three bodies were lying huddled together, evidently the work of a single shell ; and here and there were scattered groups of threes and fours, while a single corpse supported by a fence, stood up, grim in death, grasping the rusty musket which in life he was in the act of loading.

* * * * * *

By his frequent raids on territory under British jurisdiction, plundering and burning towns and villages, murdering the men and carrying off the women and children, Gbow had made himself "the terror of the Sherbro country," and it is believed that this severe lesson will have a most beneficial effect in a district where lawlessness and crime have been allowed to go unchecked far too long.

Thus ended this most successful expedition, such a salutary lesson were needed to restore order and protect life ; and, to punish a man who had suddenly forced himself into notoriety and dangerous power by his bravery and relentless cruelty, it was carried out with a completeness and thoroughness deserving of the highest commendation.

This expedition was followed by another one a week later, which pushed far into the interior of the Sherbro district, but there was little or no fighting on the part of the soldiers and police. The *Standard* correspondent thus describes it :—

Following the successful campaign up the Small Boom River, which resulted in the destruction of Gbow's strongholds with great loss of life, a third expedition was sent from Sherbro for the purpose of encouraging the allies in the destruction of the remaining towns in Gbow's territory, and also to convince the native tribes and their turbulent chiefs by an armed demonstration that the Government were able to reach them in their fever-stricken creeks and rivers. The force detailed for the purpose consisted of one Company of the 2nd West India Regiment, under Captain Skelton and Lieut. Dunn, and eighty rank and file of the Constabulary under Captain Jackson and Mr. Revington. The Administrator, Mr. Pinkett, the Acting-Civil Commandant, Mr. Laborch, and Mr. Jarrett, accompanied the expedition. The Colonial steamer "Prince of Wales," having in tow the boats filled with the troops, left Sherbro early on the morning of the 7th June and steamed down the Shebar River. Through the courtesy of the Agent of the French Compagnie du Senegal, who own large stores in the district, a steam launch of light draught was placed at the disposal of the Government, and proved most useful, as it towed the large boats containing the supplies and ammunition necessary for the expedition. The "Prince of Wales," owing to her draught, was unable to proceed past Shebar; the thirty-two boats were accordingly manned, and, the breeze being favourable, sails were hoisted, the bugle sounded the "Advance," and we were soon skimming along the Big Boom and Kettam River. The estuary was about three miles wide at this part; and the scene presented was an animated and picturesque one, as the flotilla of boats, full of armed men in bright uniforms spread over the narrow expanse of water sparkling in the morning sun, the low river banks, covered with mangrove bush, on the roots of which clusters of oysters grow in profusion, and the monotonous background occasionally relieved by the stately palm.

A sudden change, however, soon occurred; a dark mass

of black clouds appeared on the horizon, and rapidly approached towards us, while sheet and forked lightning of great vividness flashed through the lowering sky, followed by peal after peal of heavy thunder. An African tornado was upon us, and soon burst with the greatest fury. All sails were immediately struck and every endeavour made to keep the boats' heads to the swollen river as it was driven past us by the storm. Rain fell in torrents for over an hour, when the sky again cleared, and the sun made its welcome appearance, and soon dried our soaked clothes as we again proceeded on our journey. Gbap was reached about five o'clock, and our unexpected arrival caused considerable excitement and commotion. On landing, to our surprise, a salute of twelve guns was fired from some old nine-pounders, which had been obtained many years previously; and as doubts had been expressed as to Pah Tucker's sincerity to the Government this act of loyalty gave the Administrator considerable satisfaction. However, it was afterwards ascertained that this salute was intended to warn the enemy of our approach, and we felt humiliated and annoyed at being so easily and completely duped by this wary chief's artifice. The town is defended by a double stockade, contains between two and three thousand inhabitants, and is under British protection; the houses consist of the usual mud huts of conical shape, which appear to be general to all African tribes on the West Coast.

At daybreak we continued up the rapidly narrowing river against a very strong current, but, the breeze being still favourable, by dint of sails and hard pulling, the rate of advance was fairly maintained. Nothing of interest occurred to relieve the monotony other than occasional tropical birds and the annoyance from the repeated attacks of the mangrove fly, the bite of which is most painful; and the order to halt at Toom was gladly obeyed. On landing, the town was found to be deserted, the inhabitants having fled from fear of Gbow, who had pillaged and burnt a small town close by. A few miles above Toom we came to the barmouth, as the junction of the Big Boom and Kittam Rivers is called, and proceeded up the Big Boom proper. Shortly after entering it a marked improvement in the country begins, the low mangrove-bound lines giving way to high banks and rich alluvial fields, covered with luxuriant grass and interspersed with well-grown paddy plantations extending to the water's edge. We were now in the territory of Chief Gberri, and the men and women labouring in the fields received the passing boats with shouts of delight and satisfaction, for they could now work on their farms without dread of capture from Gbow, with whom Gberri had been carrying on a war for a long time with indifferent success until the Administrator desired to take up his cause. Barainy was reached at dusk, and is the last town under British control in the Boom country. Twenty policemen are stationed here, and they have made such primitive preparations for our comfort as the district could furnish. For the first time for several days we enjoyed the luxury of sitting at a table, a welcome change from the seat of a boat or the dung-laid floors of the native huts. The town was full of native allies, and, being now sure of a base for their operations, they set out against the enemy, whom they defeated and routed without any assistance, burning and pillaging their towns and making prisoners of the women and children they captured, not one single man being brought in.

Next day Commendeh was reached, and consisted of two towns, the new and the old, and was strongly fortified by four rows of stockades opening one into the other. This is the principal town of Gberri, and a halt was made for two days, during which time reports were received of the successes of the Mendis, who drove Gbow's war-boys completely from the country. The expeditionary force accordingly started on the journey down river, and at the barmouth it was considered advisable that the soldiers should return to Sherbro, while the Administrator and civil officers, with the Constabulary, proceeded up the Kittam River to Camalay, to conclude a treaty with Queen Messee, of Massah, for the cession of her territory..... Queen Messee's territory extends from Camalay to the Gallinas country, recently annexed, and secures to the colony an unbroken coast line from Cape Sierra Leone to the Gallinas Point. After the usual palaver, at Massah, and the signing of the treaty, the Administrator distributed the presents to the Queen and her followers. The Queen appeared extremely proud of her attire, being robed in a long bath towel and an ordinary English-made tall hat, which she only wears on state occasions. She held in her hand an elephant's tail, encased in a massive silver holder. After bidding farewell to our new subjects the boats were manned and the return journey began. At Barmany the police succeeded in capturing Bey Yormah, who was nominal king over Gbow's territory, and Gbap, Pah Tucker, and Chief Tongofoorah were made prisoners, Tucker thus being caught red-handed in league with the enemy, as Tongofoorah was head warrior to Gbow, and had fought with great bravery at Talliah, where he had been wounded. This concluded the third expedition against Gbow, who has been driven completely from the country.

As a demonstration this expedition was of extreme use, for the peaceable natives returned to their work, while those who had been living by plunder and murder realised that they were not safe from punishment, as they had supposed, even in the depths of these fever stricken rivers and creeks.

The effect of these expeditions was to bring back Governor Havelock as soon as his short leave expired, and, under his masterly tact, law, and order were soon restored, and the colony once more proceeded in the even tenor of its sickly life.

CHAPTER XXII.

A GHOST—SNAKES—AND UNPLEASANT DUTIES.

THE gallant 2nd West were in a curious state of mind; one of the rooms in the officers' barracks was declared to be haunted, and, although the officers pooh-poohed it, they all took the first opportunity of getting away from the undesirable room. Hence the last arrival from leave, unless he was of sufficient rank to kick out some poor junior, generally occupied it. They each in turn had some graphic experience to relate: " that, in the still night, a cold shadowless substance seemed to pass over the body or the face, leaving a clammy unpleasant sensation behind." On mess nights the subject was the invariable topic of conversation, and the man in occupation of the room for the time being had to endure a good deal of cross-questioning as to the last actions of the ghostly visitor.

Without exaggeration, more than a dozen officers had testified to the ghost, and unbelievers, after a few days' trial, were only too glad to go back to their own rooms again, though it was generally admitted that the ghost was somewhat erratic in its movements. One officer, with an evident leaning to the unknown and mysterious, detailed in thrilling words how he had been awakened in the night and felt a chill hand like that of the dead passing slowly and softly over his face as though endeavouring to feel his features. He struck a light as quickly as possible, and there was nothing whatever to be seen, the room was in its usual state and not a thing moved. And his experiences differed but slightly from that of the others. Sub-lieutenants, lieutenants, doctors, captains, all positively declared that they had been disturbed by this unknown damp hand, and the subject threatened to develop itself into one of the mysteries of haunted experiences.

This room was not situated in a quiet corner of the barracks, but in its very centre on the principal floor, and only separated from the mess by the passage leading to the staircase, so the ghost had not selected any quiet spot for his visitation. However, one night a surgeon who had the ill luck to be in possession of the mysterious chamber, and who was most emphatic in the belief of the presence of something as yet undiscovered, returned to it after an absence of a few days in the hills. Just as he was going to step into bed he heard a hissing sound proceeding from it, and to his horror saw a large black snake ready to dispute possession. The snake got the best of it, for a few seconds, for the medico retreated yelling out for help; then he rushed to the corner of the room and drew his sword as a lot of fellows came tumbling in from the mess.

They were not a moment too soon, for the snake had made its way off the bed to a large cupboard, behind which it was rapidly wriggling, when a well-aimed blow severed it in two. It was a black-headed cobra over three feet in length, and very thick. Its fangs were found to be full of deadly poison, and its bite would have been fatal, certainly within two hours, to any of the many fellows with whom it had chummed. It seems wonderful that none of them should have been bitten, for they had at different times tried to discover who their clammy companion was. Behind the cupboard a small hole was found leading below the flooring, and thither the serpent had been in the habit of retiring by day, while in the night it came out to seek the pleasant companionship and warmth of a human bedfellow.

The colony is infested with snakes, from the python to the bright little snake of dazzling green that glides harmlessly across the paths of the unfrequented fields. Deaths by snake-poisoning are, however, very rare, as a snake will always get away if he can. The Africans are unlike the Indians with regard to snakes, dreading them almost as much as they do alligators, while snake-charmers are almost unknown among them. One of these men, however, came down to Sierra Leone from the far interior, but he fell a victim to his precarious trade. He had been exhibiting his snakes, and going through the usual performances, while we looked on doubtingly at what we believed to be a harmless exhibition. One of his snakes was a black-headed cobra, but we believed, despite the man's assertion to the contrary, that the poisonous fangs had been withdrawn. However, he continued his performances about the town and in the low public-houses, where he got rather intoxicated. Whether he irritated the cobra too much while in this condition, or the cobra disliked the smell of alcohol, only the snake could have decided, but it bit the wretched man, and in less than an hour he was lying dead in the colonial surgeon's house, where but a few hours before he had been performing for our gratification.

Our colonial surgeon was somewhat of a snake-fancier, and it was astonishing to see how rapidly the snakes grew in size and strength. The manner in which they kill and eat their prey is peculiar. With one dart the wretched dog or fowl would be killed, and the snake would then salivate the part it could get its mouth over. The body would next be twirled over the head and turned round the food two or three times, and thus crushing it as small as the strength of the snake's body would do it, while the act of swallowing would be steadily proceeded with. At first the outline of the swallowed substance could be easily traced; in a few days it would be smaller and lower down, and so on till it disappeared. Crushing the food in this way, one can easily understand how it is that small deer or kids are swallowed, horns and all, by a large-sized python. A snake not thicker than a man's small finger can swallow a rat in a very short time, and it can certainly be assumed that a snake eighteen feet long, and proportionately thick, could get outside a very big animal.

In snake-infested countries, there is a strong belief that the most poisonous snake-bite need not terminate fatally if the patient be kept moving briskly, so as not to allow the circulation to stop. An impossibility almost, one would say, the narcotic poison is so strong. But I have met a gentleman who asserts that he has brought round a native, who was in a state of coma and almost pulseless, by goading and violently rubbing him until a certain amount of vitality returned. The victim was then run up and down a long verandah by relays of men, stumbling and falling while he was kept awake by cruelties and tortures such as would have created envy in the heart of a Chinese executioner. While I cannot vouch for the authenticity of this cure, as the object to be gained is to keep the blood circulating freely it appears feasible enough; and if I were ever bitten by a poisonous snake, I should, until a safer cure is discovered, prefer this treatment to all internal medicines. Cauterisation appears to be a waste of valuable time, unless instantaneously implied, which is rarely possible unless done by the sufferer himself.

In the Police Court at times the magistrates are called upon to decide most curious cases involving local customs. One peculiar case that came before me I think is deserving of record. The complainant had taken out a summons against the defendant for the value of a sow. When the case was called, and the man duly sworn, he informed me that "he had loaned (lent) the man a sow."

"What! lent the man a sow?" I inquired, astonished.

"Yes, sah, I loaned him a sow."

'But why did you lend him a sow?"

"I loaned him sow, sah, on 'greement, and he got to gib me half de lilly ones ebery time she catch any. And he been sold it."

"And have you many sows out on loan?" I asked, interested.

"Oh, yes, sah; dat bery common here, it country fashion, but dis fellow been sold it."

"No, sah, I not sold it, it been seized for debt," interrupted the defendant.

Complainant: "It's all de same, sah. I loan him de sow, and I want de price ob it now it's sold."

"Well, my man, I can't help you in such a case. Clearly you lend the sow to the man at your own risk and for your profit, and I cannot help you."

"Please, massa, dis bery important case, and you see how full de court is to hear de decision. Plenty person here loan sows, and it's old country custom. You see, sah, I no gib de sow; I loan it only, and if I like I can take it back again, and dis man been sold it, and I want de value."

"Now, how many little pigs did you get from this sow?" I asked.

"Twenty-one, sah. He been had de sow many years, and feed it, and we been half de picken."

"Has there been any similar case to this?" I asked the clerk.

"No, sir, but nearly all the sows are lent out that way."

"Well, my man, you can come again to-morrow when the magistrate returns, but I do not think you have any case. Why not settle it out of court between yourselves?"

I mentioned the matter to the legal adviser, but he declined giving any legal opinion on local customs, and the magistrate had great difficulty in satisfying the pig-owner that he had no legal claim for his lost sow.

The management of the gaol gave much trouble to Governor Havelock, for the colony could not afford to pay for an officer of sufficient responsibility to manage it. Consequently the senior officials were appointed as visiting justices, and had to attend in turns and inspect the gaol and daily settle the quarrels and complaints constantly made by or against the prisoners. Such work was most trying and disagreeable, and as it had to be done out of office hours, it pressed very hardly upon the officers.

The gaol was full of bad characters, made worse by the impossibility of maintaining discipline among them, owing to the unsuitability of the building. There were no less than five murderers expiating their crimes in long sentences. But these were well-conducted prisoners in comparison with others who seemed to delight in setting all authority at defiance. The very worst character was a West India soldier—a powerful, hulking negro—who had been flogged and imprisoned in every gaol in the West Indies, and his presence in the Sierra Leone gaol threatened to bring its entire management to a deadlock. Hardly a day passed after his incarceration but that he was brought up for some offence of discipline, and punishment and low diet seemed only to afford him a pretext for refusing to do the one, and expressing himself quite satisfied with the other.

His offence had been a military one, and when he was marched down to the gaol, while waiting to be handed over to the civil authorities, he cut his uniform into pieces in the coolest way, the escort declining to interfere. At last, for seriously threatening one of the warders, I sentenced him to twenty-five lashes, which received the Governor's approval. His behaviour before me was so threatening, that at the end of my week's work I cautioned the succeeding visiting justice to be careful, as I felt convinced the man meant mischief. My caution was only too well founded, for he was up again on the first day, notwithstanding that my punishment had not been administered. After his case was gone into, he was marched back to the work-yard and given a hammer to break stones. Instead of which he violently assaulted the warders, chasing them round the yard, all of them running away, while the other prisoners looked on without interfering. There was a small military guard in the yard, not one of whom considered it a part of his duty to arrest the prisoner. The keeper of the gaol, hearing the disturbance, entered the work-yard, and although he had only just risen from a bed of sickness, and was still suffering from fever, he boldly endeavoured to take the hammer away. The prisoner allowed him to get fairly close, and then suddenly flung the heavy hammer at him, but it whizzed past his head. The prisoner next rushed up to the sentry on duty and snatched the rifle from his hands, and, clubbing it, again attacked the plucky gaoler. Swinging the rifle round his head, he aimed a blow which would certainly have been fatal to the unfortunate man, but his fever stood him in good stead, for in trying to close with the prisoner, he slipped and half fell, the weapon descending with a crash on the hard ground. The stock of the rifle was smashed, and the barrel bent nearly double from the force of the blow, and the infuriated ruffian fell headlong to the ground from having missed the object aimed at. The head gaoler then threw himself on the prisoner, and, the warders coming up, he was secured with much difficulty. All this time the military guard stood looking on, declining to render the slightest assistance, although they were called upon several times by the gaoler to do so. For this attack the man was tried before the civil authorities, and received an additional long term of imprisonment, but as he absolutely refused to work, his punishment was not a very severe one.

Governor Havelock was going away for a few months, and, during his absence, Mr. Tarleton, who was acting judge, was to administer, while a dormant commission was also made out for me as judge, so that I should be available to administer the Government in the event of any accident to Mr. Tarleton. At the time I was acting as colonial secretary, and my health was in a very serious state from repeated attacks of fever. But the colony was very shorthanded, and, although my leave was overdue, I readily agreed to continue until the Governor returned. During his absence things went anything but smoothly, and it was with the greatest difficulty that the work was kept going. Unknown to us all, and even to himself, the acting governor was suffering from a serious internal malady which quite upset his reason, and from which he succumbed a few months afterwards. In consequence of this, he entered into the most violent antagonism with the natives, especially his council, and day after day, though utterly unfit for work, I had to arrange matters pacifically, so as to prevent serious local troubles. As acting judge, he had proceeded to Sherbro, and there condemned a man for a murder upon the very weakest of evidence. In council, reduced only to the acting governor, the officer commanding the troops, and myself, I earnestly appealed on behalf of the fellow's life; the officer commanding, Colonel Talbot, did likewise; while an influential petition was signed by the leading natives and English residents on the wretched man's behalf, but without avail. Mr. Tarleton, as governor, declined to extend his powers of clemency to the man that Mr. Tarleton, as judge, had condemned.

To my dismay, I received peremptory instructions that, as acting colonial secretary and senior visiting justice, I should be held responsible for the proper conduct of the execution. In vain I appealed and argued; in vain I pointed out that there was a sheriff, and such was his duty and not mine. I was ordered to superintend all the arrangements, since a mad idea seemed to possess the acting governor that the sentence would be bungled so as to get him into a row. Day after day I had to visit the doomed wretch, who each time assured me of his entire innocence in reply to my questions as to whether he wanted anything. Though I had never seen a gallows, I was held responsible for its safety, and at last the day arrived when the man was led forth, and, after declaring his innocence, the wretched work was completed, but not until I had left the precincts of the scene.

This sickening duty was the last straw to my health in its then enfeebled condition, and I can only write of an indistinct remembrance of a sick-bed, a few kind visitors, the return of our stalwart colonial surgeon from leave, a hasty examination, a hurried packing and a crowded vessel, hand-shakings and good-byes, and I was at sea, steaming away rapidly from the "white man's grave," cheating it out of one addition to the thousands already buried beneath its pestilential sands.

CHAPTER XXIII.

HOMEWARD BOUND.

OF the first few days at sea I knew nothing, but it gradually dawned on me that I was in the end cabin near the propeller, which went racing round with racking noise as we pitched in the teeth of the life-giving trades. The berth above mine was also occupied, and as my head became clearer, fellow passengers, many of whom were known to me, visited me to cheer me up. The ship was very crowded, and the only berth that could be found for me was the uncomfortable one I occupied.

While my understanding became clearer, my strength gradually diminished, and the doctor was a repeated visitor. But a day came when he was accompanied by the Captain, and presently the Bishop, who was also a passenger, entered the cabin. After a few minutes I saw for what they had come. It wanted no adroit questioning. I gave the addresses of friends at home, and, an inventory having been made, my possessions were handed over to the Captain, who, after a few cherry remarks, left with the doctor.

There was no doubt the fever was a bad one. For days I had been violently seized with ague, which even quinine seemed powerless to touch. Neither hot-water bottles nor blankets were of any avail, and nothing would stop the numb chattering movement, while fingers and lips and eyelids turned a livid hue, as the body was shaken like an aspen-leaf. Later in the day came the hot burning stage, with an all-consuming fire eating up my very life, to be followed by profuse sweating, when my attenuated frame was wrung as though a wet sponge. Yes, I was bad, and knew that it was more than doubtful whether I should ever see land again, and that the deep sea, but a few miles from where we were steaming, would be my last resting place.

I said good-bye to the kindly Bishop, and took one more strong dose of quinine, for I did not believe in caving in. What are one's thoughts on such occasions? How one's life passes in review order slowly through one's brain—the childhood spent in travel, the school with its triumphs of cricket and prizes, the friends of after years, the voyage out to the coast, full of life, hope, and interest, and the sunshine and shade of my tropical days, all passed before me as a panorama of the shadowy past, to be ended in a few short hours, I thought, as I dropped into a sound sleep.

"I am awake again. But what are they doing? Shall I shout, to show that I am not dead? Yes—no—I will lie still and see what they are up to. Won't they be sold when they find I am not even asleep!" But I was being lifted quietly, and was carried through the dimly lighted saloon and deposited in another cabin, and I heard the doctor distinctly saying "He will do there." So I turned over and slept again, determined to inquire all about it in the morning.

"What are those subdued voices?" I said to myself. "Oh, from the saloon." I found, on opening my eyes, the glorious light of a bright sunny morning sent its dancing beams into the cabin of life. "Why, where am I?" were my first thoughts. My berth was certainly against the ship's side, and here I was against the panelling of the saloon. Then it dawned upon me that I had been moved in the night, and how much more comfortable the change was!

"Steward, coffee—steward, cocoa; and please bring me some more bread and butter." The early risers were taking their first meal evidently. "Poor fellow, he's gone at last," I heard a voice say. "Dear me, who's dead?" I wondered. "Yes, he was very bad yesterday, and handed over," someone else added. "I suppose they thought I was too ill to tell me," I considered to myself. "Perhaps I am in the poor fellow's cabin."

"Among his things he had rather a peculiar ring," continued the first speaker. "Who can it be? I, too, had a peculiar African ring." Then I became curious—I must find out who had died. Inquisitiveness is certainly an invalid's weakness. So I crawled out of the bunk, and with a blanket round me for warmth I managed to enter the saloon.

"Good morning," I said.

"Good heavens! Why, wh—wh—where did you come from? We thought—oh—ah—yes—sit down here old fellow. Have some cocoa, eh? I am so glad to see that you are better."

"Oh, you are surprised to see me coming out of that cabin? Well, they moved me into it during the night."

"Oh, yes, that's it. I could not understand you coming out of that cabin," was the answer.

"Who's dead?" I asked.

"Who's dead?" was the rejoinder.

"I thought I heard you talking of somebody who had died in the night?"

"N—n—n—not at all—n—n—no one has died that I know of."

Then the doctor came in, and I was ordered back to bed again. But there had been no return of ague, and I was on the mend at last. We had passed Goree, and, a passenger having disembarked there, I was moved into his cabin during the night unknown to anyone but the doctor and sailors who had assisted him. In the morning my cabin companion had leant over his berth to ask how I was, and seeing it empty had concluded it was all over, and had mentioned it to the other passengers as the "early coffee news."

No thoughts of landing at any of the intermediate ports in my case. One by one they were passed, and at last the joyous words, "homeward bound," were on all lips. From the cabin boy to the captain all were cheery and happy, "for were not the girls pulling at the ropes," a sailor's expression, meaning that the ship is "nearing home."

Once more among friends, to be nursed through another bout of fever. But I pulled through again, and the buoyancy of life and strength were gradually restored as the months passed by, bringing round the time when I must again start for "the white man's grave." There, the hand of death had been busy indeed. Never more should I see the kindly doctor whose timely arrival saved my life, for his body lies deep in the Atlantic between Teneriffe and Madeira. Gone also is his cherry assistant, who, against his better judgment, allowed me to continue on long after repeated attacks of fever had shown that it was at the risk of life. And down in the fathomless sea lies the late acting governor, who also succumbed on his way home, while in the cemetery many newly-made mounds proved that the sickly season had once more claimed a heavy percentage of human life.

At last my leave was up, and I reported myself for return. But the medical examination was unsatisfactory, and in such circumstances the Colonial Office would not sanction my going. So I bade farewell to Sierra Leone, wondering whether at some future date official duty would again land me as a toiler on its fever-stricken shores.

THE END.

CHAS. STRAKER AND SONS, PRINTERS, BISHOPSGATE AVENUE, LONDON; AND REDHILL.

www.ingramcontent.com/pod-product-compliance
Lightning Source LLC
Chambersburg PA
CBHW022041230426
43672CB00008B/1031